MICROSOFT® EXCEL® FOR STOCK AND OPTION TRADERS

MICROSOFT® EXCEL® FOR STOCK AND OPTION TRADERS

BUILD YOUR OWN ANALYTICAL TOOLS FOR HIGHER RETURNS

JEFF AUGEN

Vice President, Publisher: Tim Moore
Associate Publisher and Director of Marketing: Amy Neidlinger
Executive Editor: Jim Boyd
Editorial Assistant: Pamela Boland
Operations Manager: Gina Kanouse
Senior Marketing Manager: Julie Phifer
Publicity Manager: Laura Czaja
Assistant Marketing Manager: Megan Colvin
Cover Designer: Chuti Prasertsith
Managing Editor: Kristy Hart
Project Editor: Betsy Harris
Copy Editor: Cheri Clark
Proofreader: Kathy Ruiz
Indexer: Erika Millen
Senior Compositor: Gloria Schurick
Manufacturing Buyer: Dan Uhrig

© 2011 by Pearson Education, Inc.
Publishing as FT Press
Upper Saddle River, New Jersey 07458

FT Press offers excellent discounts on this book when ordered in quantity for bulk purchases or special sales. For more information, please contact U.S. Corporate and Government Sales, 1-800-382-3419, corpsales@pearsontechgroup.com. For sales outside the U.S., please contact International Sales at international@pearson.com.

Company and product names mentioned herein are the trademarks or registered trademarks of their respective owners.

Printed in the United States of America

First Printing April 2011

ISBN-10: 0-13-713182-8
ISBN-13: 978-0-13-713182-2

Pearson Education LTD.
Pearson Education Australia PTY, Limited.
Pearson Education Singapore, Pte. Ltd.
Pearson Education North Asia, Ltd.
Pearson Education Canada, Ltd.
Pearson Educación de Mexico, S.A. de C.V.
Pearson Education—Japan
Pearson Education Malaysia, Pte. Ltd.

Library of Congress Cataloging-in-Publication Data

Augen, Jeffrey.

Microsoft Excel for stock and option traders : build your own analytical tools for higher returns / Jeffrey Augen.

p. cm.

ISBN 978-0-13-713182-2 (hbk. : alk. paper)

1. Investment analysis—Computer programs. 2. Investment analysis—Mathematical models. 3. Microsoft Excel (Computer file) I. Title.

HG4515.5.A94 2011

332.640285'554—dc22

2011003034

*To Lisa, who changed everything when she said:
"Why don't you just calculate the integral between
those two points and chart the value as
it changes over time?"*

Contents

Acknowledgments

I would like to thank the team that helped pull the book together. First must be Jim Boyd, who encouraged me to continue the project and always seems willing to explore new areas and concepts. This book would never have made it to print without advice and direction from Jim. Once again it was my pleasure to work with Betsy Harris, who always does a terrific job turning a rough manuscript into a polished, production-quality book. In that regard, I must also thank Cheri Clark, who carefully read every word and made corrections that put the finishing touch on the work. Finally, I'd like to acknowledge the important contributions of a friend—Robert Birnbaum. Over the past several months, Robert has helped shape my thinking about the statistical relevance of trends—ideas which surfaced in some of the key examples and continue to weigh heavily in my own investing.

About the Author

J eff Augen, currently a private investor and writer, has spent more than a decade building a unique intellectual property portfolio of databases, algorithms, and associated software for technical analysis of derivatives prices. His work, which includes more than a million lines of computer code, is particularly focused on the identification of subtle anomalies and price distortions.

Augen has a 25-year history in information technology. As cofounding executive of IBM's Life Sciences Computing business, he defined a growth strategy that resulted in $1.2 billion of new revenue and managed a large portfolio of venture capital investments. From 2002 to 2005, Augen was President and CEO of TurboWorx Inc., a technical computing software company founded by the chairman of the Department of Computer Science at Yale University. His books include *Trading Realities*, *Day Trading Options*, *Trading Options at Expiration*, *The Option Trader's Workbook*, and *The Volatility Edge in Options Trading*. He currently teaches option trading classes at the New York Institute of Finance and writes a weekly column for *Stocks, Futures and Options* magazine.

Preface

In August 2010, Cisco stock (ticker: CSCO) hovered just a few cents below $25. Several analysts identified the stock as a strong buy. They pointed to the rising demand for network infrastructure that, among other things, was being driven by explosive growth in online video gaming and Internet television. Cisco, they believed, would continue to dominate the consumer market while benefiting from a weak dollar and low manufacturing costs. They must have been wrong because the stock fell 15% when earnings were released on August 11. The price continued to decline until August 31, when it bottomed out at $19—24% below its previous high. About the time that everyone had given up and turned bearish, the stock began to rally. On November 10 the price was, once again, back up to $24.50. Then came another earnings report and another sharp decline. The price immediately fell 16% and continued plunging until, on December 3, it once again bottomed out at $19. These bizarre dynamics played out a third time, with the stock rallying steadily to $22 on February 9, 2011, before falling back to $18.92 the very next day after earnings were released—another 14% decline. Figure P.1 displays Cisco closing prices from June 1, 2010, to February 11, 2011.

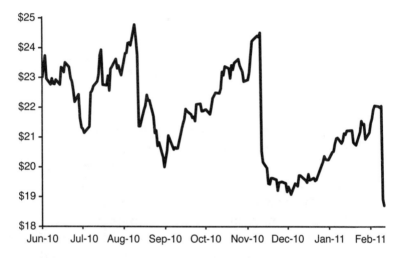

FIGURE P.1   *CSCO closing prices June 1, 2010 to February 11, 2011.*

Wild unpredictability doesn't seem to discourage speculators because the trading volume for Cisco remains shockingly high. Moreover, the number of investors who bet on the direction of the stock seems to peak just before and after earnings—the most dangerous times of all. For example, the trading volume climbed above 125 million shares on February 9, 2011 (before earnings), and skyrocketed to 560 million shares the next day after the numbers were released. Each of the previously outlined events was accompanied by a similar pattern of extremely high volume the day before earnings were announced and even higher volume the day after.

Who would trade this completely unpredictable stock? Why does the volume soar at the most dangerous times when anything seems possible? More importantly, why do analysts believe that they know enough to make predictions? The answers are simple. Analysts can make all the predictions they want because it's not their money that ends up being lost, and speculators always believe they can find a bargain. As a group, investors tend to be arrogant. They typically believe that they have unique insights and that these insights give them an advantage over the market. One of the most common mistakes is relying on traditional off-the-shelf technical indicators that often prove to be even less reliable than fundamental analysis. The Cisco story represents one of the best examples of the problem.

Various technical indicators signaled that the stock would continue to rally just before each of the sharp declines displayed in Figure P.1. They were clearly wrong. Moreover, technical indicators cannot be valid if the underlying trend being analyzed is statistically insignificant. Yet technical analysts routinely talk about moving-average crosses, momentum, or relative strength, without any reference to the statistical strength of the underlying trend being studied. We can compile the relevant statistics for any stock in just a few seconds by loading the information into a spreadsheet and applying Excel's r-squared function. Not surprisingly, the test reveals that most trends appearing on stock charts have very low statistical significance. For Cisco, a relatively weak r-squared value of 0.7 is achieved less than 30% of the time using a 10-day sliding window. Highly significant trends with r-squared values above 0.9 occur with a frequency less than 5%. Table P.1 displays r-squared data for 2 years of Cisco stock.

TABLE P.1   *Compiled r-squared values for Cisco stock February 2009 to February 2011. Calculations span a 10-day sliding window.*

	rsq>.9	rsq>.8	rsq>.7	rsq>.6	rsq>.5
Days	24	96	146	189	238
Percent	4.8%	19.4%	29.5%	38.2%	48.1%

The table is divided into columns that reveal the number and percentage of days appearing in trends with minimum r-squared values listed in the column headings. In some sense the data represents a dose of reality. It is common, for example, to hear a technical analyst turn bullish because the 50-day moving average has crossed above the 200-day moving average. However, it is unlikely that you will ever hear the same analyst report the r-squared value of the current trendline. Fortunately, however, most good trading platforms have an r-squared function that can display on a chart, and the data can be exported to a spreadsheet where more detailed analysis can be used to study different length windows and combinations of indicators. This kind of analysis can be used to validate, invalidate, or tune combinations of indicators and give investors an edge against the market. In today's complex computer-driven markets, this kind of analysis can make the difference between winning and losing.

Modern trading platforms always include sophisticated tools for back-testing indicators and strategies. But before a strategy can be tested, it must first be developed, and that development is best accomplished on a foundation of statistical analysis. Spreadsheets and databases are the perfect platform for that kind of technical work. In most cases the process involves a sequence of basic questions designed to reveal the statistical behavior of a stock following a specific set of conditions. There is virtually no limit to the size, number, or complexity of the experiments that can be performed to search for unique correlations that are not generally known to the market.

This book is designed to help technically minded private investors learn to run just a little faster than the market. A few years ago the discussion would have been too complex to be generally useful because it would have been focused on data mining strategies in large databases. That has all changed. Most of the complex statistical analysis and model building that a few years ago could only be accomplished at the institutional level is now within the reach of any investor with a trading platform and a copy of Microsoft Excel. This book is built on that theme. It is designed to help investors learn to translate complex questions into simple spreadsheet models. The discussions span a range from simple conditionals and logical expressions to relatively complex VBA programs that generate statistical summary tables. My goal was to include content that can add value to the efforts of a wide range of investors and to challenge everyone to improve their analytical capabilities.

Chapter 1

Introduction—
The Value of Information

The Struggle for a Statistical Edge

The equities markets are a zero sum game in the sense that every dollar won must also be lost. This simple fact has far-reaching implications that are sometimes counterintuitive. For example, most investors do not realize that the investment community as a group cannot profit from the rise of a single stock unless the company pays a dividend. This limitation exists because all profit must emanate from buying and selling activity between the investors themselves. Although individual trades can certainly generate a positive return, there is a finite amount of money in the system and the source of that money is the individual investors. The markets are the ultimate expression of capitalism—someone always wins and someone else always loses.

The game manifests itself as a struggle between buyers and sellers. To consistently win the struggle, you must have an advantage—either technical or informational. Unfortunately, a growing population of today's investors engages in illegal insider trading. They have an undeniable advantage because they make investment decisions based on information not available to the general public. It is sometimes easy to spot insider trading activity. It often takes the form of a large purchase of inexpensive out-of-the-money options just before a surprise news announcement. Not surprisingly, many investors subscribe to fee-based services that track suspicious option trading activity. Unfortunately, the picture is colored by rumors and it is relatively difficult to capitalize on this type of information.

My introduction to the world of insider trading came many years ago, in June 1995, when IBM purchased Lotus Development Corporation. On Thursday, June 1, Lotus stock closed at $29.25, but the volume of out-of-the-money $40 strike price calls had risen from nearly zero to more than 400 contracts for no apparent reason. The trend continued on Friday, with the stock closing at $30.50 and 416 of the $40 calls trading for $3/16 (just over 18 cents).[1] On Monday, June 5, the stock closed at $32.50, and the volume of the $40 calls jumped to 1043 contracts at $9/16 (56 cents). The next day, after the announcement, the stock closed at $61.43 and the $40 strike price calls traded for $21.75—a 3800% profit. The $58,000 invested in these options the previous day was now worth nearly $2.3 million. Someone knew something and it was reflected in active trading of deep out-of-the-money, nearly worthless calls. This sort of blatantly illegal activity is far more common than most investors realize. It drives markets at all levels and takes many different forms. Investment tips from brokers to their friends about unannounced merger and acquisition activity, information leaks ahead of government reports, corporate executives who exercise options immediately before a stock decline, market timing and late trading in mutual funds, and large net-worth investors who manipulate thinly traded stocks represent a small portion of the problem. Needless to say, the financial markets are not a level playing field. Some of the most notorious examples of insider trading occurred just before the September 11, 2001, terrorist attacks when put contract volumes soared for American and United Airlines, residents of the World Trade Center (Morgan Stanley) and reinsurance companies. The German Central Bank President, Ernst Welteke, later reported, "There are ever clearer signs that there were activities on international financial markets that must have been carried out with the necessary expert knowledge."[2] Insider trading before the 9/11 attacks was not confined to stocks. The markets also saw surges in gold, oil, and 5-year U.S. Treasury Notes— each considered to be a solid investment in the event of a world crisis.

The typical investor lives at the other end of the spectrum. He is not involved in illegal insider trading and must find profit opportunities using off-the-shelf charting tools, financial news broadcasts, information available on the World Wide Web, and broker-supplied trading software. Most investors use both technical charting and fundamental analysis to make trading decisions. Some day trade while others structure longer term positions. Regardless of the approach, each investor must compete against the market (including the insiders) using information that is freely available to everyone. Advantages can be gained only by those who have unique insights or approaches that have not been discovered by their competitors. Unfortunately, a valuable insight that reliably generates profit will be short-lived if it truly represents an inefficiency in the market. Calendar effects—anomalies in stock returns that relate to the calendar—are one of the most interesting examples of this phenomenon.

Such anomalies have been the object of extensive investigation for many years. They include day, week, month, and holiday distortions. Their names are descriptive—January effect, turn-of-month effect, turn-of-quarter effect, end-of-year effect, Monday effect, and so on. In August 2000, the Federal Reserve Bank of Atlanta published a paper on the turn-of-month (TOM) effect.[3] The research was designed to address assertions by financial economists that returns are unusually large beginning on the last trading day of the month and continuing forward three trading days. S&P 500 futures contract prices were scrutinized for evidence of TOM between 1982 and 1999. The study also addressed the possibility of significant return differences across TOM days using a complex set of classification rules that incorporated day-of-week information. The report illuminates the complexity of this and similar questions. Briefly stated, TOM effects disappear after 1990 for the S&P 500 futures contract, and these results carry over to the spot market. The change occurred just after researchers began publishing papers about the phenomenon. More subtle day-of-week and time-of-day effects seemed to be related to a shift in preference from direct stock to mutual fund purchases that occurred throughout the 1990s.

The Federal Reserve Bank's study is a sharp contrast to the large number of papers that purport to reveal new trading opportunities based on calendar effects. It makes two key points:

1. Turn-of-month return patterns are constantly subject to change because they depend on highly variable market microstructure.

2. Such opportunities cannot persist once they are widely known.

The rapid disappearance of the effect following its discovery strongly supports the Efficient Market Hypothesis (EMH) first proposed by Eugene Fama in his Ph.D. thesis at the University of Chicago Graduate School of Business in the early 1960s. EMH recognizes three basic forms of efficiency:

1. *Weak-form efficiency* implies that technical analysis will not be able to consistently produce positive returns. However, the weak-form model recognizes the possibility of producing some return based on fundamental analysis of business performance and economic climate.

2. *Semi-strong efficiency* assumes that share prices adjust to publicly available information almost instantaneously, making it impossible to place profitable trades using new, publicly available information.

3. *Strong-form efficiency* is based on the assertion that share prices reflect all available information—including information known only to insiders—at any given moment in time.

Despite efforts to curb insider trading, there is considerable evidence that U.S. equity and fixed income markets are efficient at the strong-form level. This level of efficiency is sometimes misinterpreted to imply that an individual investor cannot generate positive returns. That is not the case because the performance of the overall group fits a normal distribution that contains both winners and losers. However, the likelihood of consistently winning in a perfectly efficient market is greatly diminished. Furthermore, it is possible to generate a positive return in a rising market, and to have that return erased by currency-exchange-rate changes. Such was the case during most of 2007, when American investors saw the Dow Jones Industrial Average rise steeply while European investors lost money.

Generally speaking, dollar devaluation tends to increase the price of all dollar-denominated assets, including stocks on U.S. exchanges. It is easy to confuse the effects of these increases with actual gains.

Fingerprinting the Market

To consistently generate inflation-adjusted positive returns, an investor must have a data management system that facilitates the discovery of market inefficiencies and subtle price distortions. Standard off-the-shelf charting tools cannot be used to achieve these goals in today's market because the information they generate is available to countless investors using the same tools. The chance of discovering a unique, previously unknown combination of standard indicators that provides a genuine trading advantage is very small. Moreover, as the Federal Reserve Bank of Atlanta study documented, such opportunities rapidly vanish once they are discovered. However, with the right set of data management tools, such inefficiencies can be discovered and exploited until they disappear.

Market inefficiencies can be as small as a few cents in an option price or as large as a few dollars. They can persist for seconds, minutes, hours, or months. Some take the form of complex statistical arbitrages while others are simple triggers for buying or selling. Direction-neutral volatility distortions can also represent excellent trading opportunities for an option trader. Sometimes these distortions manifest themselves as calendar effects at the level of individual securities. Figure 1.1 contains a series of relevant examples based on 5 years of price changes for the Oil Services HOLDRs exchange traded fund (OIH). Each pane of the figure displays the average price change in standard deviations tabulated by weekday for an entire year. The images are strikingly different.

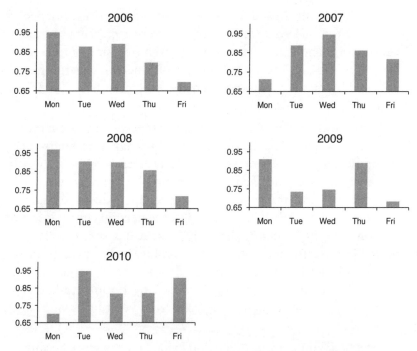

FIGURE 1.1   *Five years of price changes for the Oil Services HOLDRs (OIH) sorted by day of week. Changes are displayed in standard deviations on the y-axis; the year is marked on each pane.*

These charts represent the behavior of oil service company stocks during three distinctly different time frames. During 2006, crude prices climbed from $55 to $70 and then retreated to $55, closing the year where they began. This behavior was mirrored in 2008 when oil climbed from $88 to $135 before collapsing all the way to $32—the overall price fluctuation was larger but the outcome was the same. The 2007 chart stands out as being most different from the others. Wednesday—the day of the weekly oil-industry inventory report—was the most active in terms of price change, with Wednesday volatility rising 35% over Monday. During this year, prices climbed steadily from $51 to $85. Two of the years represented in the figure, 2009 and 2010, were characterized by rising but unstable prices. During this time frame, rapid increases were often followed by sharp corrections; sometimes as large as 10%–15% over just a couple of weeks.

Stated differently, the 2007 price-change profile is characteristic of a stable rising oil market. Monday was relatively calm; Tuesday prices represented an increased level of activity in anticipation of the Wednesday report; Wednesday was the most active; and the market steadily calmed down through Monday as it absorbed and reacted to the new inventory information. The 2007 chart, therefore, displays a sort of fingerprint for a healthy market. It has a certain level of predictability with regard to the timing of potentially large price changes—information that can be used by option traders to structure positions designed to profit from volatility swings or time decay.

The behavior evident in the 2007 chart makes sense because the weekly Energy Information Agency (EIA) Petroleum Status Report is released each Wednesday at 10:30 a.m. Eastern Standard Time. Options implied volatility tends to follow the profile of the figure, rising just before the report and declining after. However, the implied volatility increases are typically too small to compensate put and call sellers for the increased risk they take during the early part of the week, and the return to normal volatility is relatively slow. Conversely, options tend to be slightly overpriced on Friday until the close, when implied volatility shrinks as an offset to weekend time decay. Purchasing straddles near the market close on Friday and closing them after the Wednesday announcement is an excellent strategy that leverages both swings in implied volatility and knowledge gained from the chart. This particular distortion persists because it is direction-neutral and related to a specific recurring event. It directly affects implied volatility, not the price of the underlying security. Although direction-neutral anomalies are difficult to exploit by trading the stock itself, option traders can often take advantage of the mispriced volatility. There are many moving parts to the analysis, and a trader must take into account daily implied volatility, rate of time decay for each week in the expiration cycle, spacing of the strike prices, and the recent behavior of the stock. The chart provides a helpful edge.

In this way, identifying and tracking a market fingerprint can provide a statistical advantage that can be used to generate steady profits. The time frame that follows the 2007 chart—that is, 2008–2010, involves large currency swings, political upheaval, a housing/banking collapse, and ultimately a sovereign-nation debt crisis in several European countries. Trading oil or oil service company stocks during this time frame was tantamount to trading currencies, interest rates, and several other complex dynamics. Once again, the fingerprint was helpful in the sense that it steered cautious investors away from an unhealthy and difficult market. It also helped more aggressive investors recognize the importance of hedging their positions and provided valuable information about the relative strength of the required hedge. Gold-mining companies use such strategies to protect themselves against large corrections during times of instability. When the market is rising steadily and volatility is falling, they close their hedges; when they sense that the market is becoming unstable—even if it is rising—they reopen their hedges. Private investors who learn to recognize instability in the form of unusual market fingerprints can pursue similar strategies.

Creating Figure 1.1 involved the following steps:

1. One year of closing prices and dates were downloaded from a subscription-based data service into a blank Excel spreadsheet.

2. The standard deviation of the price changes was calculated using a 20-day sliding window. This information was added to each line of the table (note that the first window containing 20 price changes ends on day 21).

3. Using this information, the value of a one standard deviation price change for each day was calculated and added to the table.

4. Excel's weekday function was used to generate a single-digit number corresponding to the day of the week for each entry in the table.

5. Records were sorted and grouped according to day-of-week information.

6. The average price change in standard deviations was calculated using the sorted information.

7. Excel's charting function was used to create the figures.

A more sophisticated approach involves searching a database of thousands of stocks for ones that contain such a distortion. The database can be created using virtually any contemporary system—Microsoft Access is an excellent choice because it has virtually unlimited capacity for this kind of work, runs efficiently on a desktop machine, supports a relatively simple but powerful object-oriented programming language (Access VBA), and integrates cleanly with Excel.

Together the two software packages can form the basis of a very powerful data mining infrastructure for private investors.

The database/spreadsheet approach involves automating both the search process and calculations by writing simple programs and macros. Such a system will also facilitate the creation of custom filters for selecting stocks that meet various criteria that further define the distortion. It is possible, for example, to select stocks where the largest and smallest average daily price spikes differ by more than a preselected amount. A very powerful data mining system can be created with a limited amount of programming skill.

As we have seen, calendar effects can also manifest themselves at the broad market level. Sometimes this information can be combined with data about an individual security to gain a competitive edge. For example, the overall stock market varies slightly with regard to the size of a typical price change that is experienced for each trading day of the week. Overall, the smallest relative change—measured in standard deviations—occurs on Monday, and the largest change on Tuesday. That result is not surprising because there is less business news over the weekend for the market to react to. The differences are subtle but significant for an option trader trying to predict fair implied volatility. Figure 1.2A displays approximately 1,000 days of price-change history for the S&P 500 calculated in standard deviations. The chart begins in January 2007 and continues through the end of December 2010.

The profile has changed substantially over the past few years. Figure 1.2B displays 1,000 days of price-change history ending in October 2007.

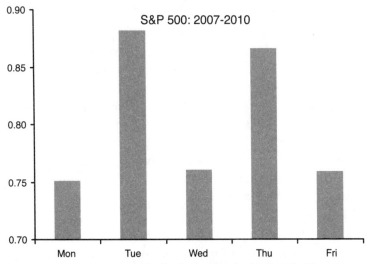

FIGURE 1.2A   *Average price spike by day for the S&P 500. Changes are measured in standard deviations against a 20-day sliding volatility window and tabulated across 1,000 trading days spanning 2007–2010.*

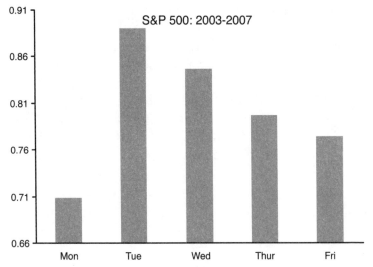

FIGURE 1.2B   *Average price spike by day for the S&P 500. Changes are measured in standard deviations against a 20-day sliding volatility window and tabulated across 1,000 trading days spanning 2003–2007.*

Both time frames are characterized by a relatively calm Monday and a much more active Tuesday. However, the rest of the profile is distinctly different. Before 2008, it was common for the largest price change of the week to occur on Tuesday, followed by a steady decrease in activity through Friday. Explosive growth in algorithmic trading, the infamous housing/banking collapse, two very large stimulus packages, a market rebound, and several large corrections followed the earlier time frame. Whatever the root causes, the new market profile (Figure 1.2A) is characterized by alternating active and calm days. This information, although subtle, is invaluable to option traders who often structure positions designed to profit from rising and falling volatility. The rising and falling market activity evident in Figure 1.2A is mirrored in implied volatility across most heavily traded optionable stocks. Some of the changes are also likely to be related to the rapid rise in popularity of weekly options. This new dynamic encourages large institutional traders to structure very short-term positions that expire each week. It also causes stocks to gravitate to and stabilize around a strike price each week. If, however, a stock is trading far from a strike on Thursday morning, buying and selling pressure often causes large moves which then stabilize the next day as expiration approaches. Charting price changes in standard deviations and parsing the results according to weekday is a simple and powerful approach to understanding and predicting behavior of individual equities and indexes. Excel is a perfect platform for this kind of analysis.

Unlike the S&P 500 and OIH, some stocks exhibit their largest price spikes on Monday because they are strongly affected by world events that transpire while the U.S. equity markets are closed over the weekend. It is sometimes possible to spot subtle distortions in the implied volatilities of options on such stocks, and to trade against these distortions before the market closes on Friday. Stocks that trade on other exchanges, such as Shanghai and Hong Kong, are particularly excellent candidates for this kind of trading.

With the appropriate infrastructure of databases and related software in place, it is possible to construct a library of calendar-based price-change charts. Results can be tabulated by day, week, month, quarter, or any other time frame that makes sense. Securities can be grouped according to a variety of criteria—industry group, price range, historical volatility, trading volume, market capitalization, short interest, and so forth. The most sophisticated designs will also include customized query tools that can be used to answer a variety of historical questions. It is also necessary to recalculate calendar-based information on a regular basis because, as we just saw, the profiles change. We will return to this discussion in various forms as we explore different approaches to data mining and feature identification in large datasets.

Just a few years ago this type of analysis would have required advanced database skills and programming tools. Much of that has changed with the dramatic increases in the speed and capacity of today's spreadsheet programs. Excel 2010 worksheets can exceed 1,000,000 rows and 16,384 columns. Just 3 years before this book was written, prior to the launch of Excel 2007, the limits were 65,536 rows and 256 columns.

Graphical Approaches to Discovering Price-Change Relationships

Whereas calendar anomalies are relatively simple to discover through trial and error, more subtle and complex relationships can be identified using automated data mining experiments that systematically execute large numbers of comparisons across different time frames. Well-constructed data mining experiments have the potential to reveal subtle relationships that are unknown to the market. Some take the form of statistically significant links between securities; others are more abstract. The software must be intelligent enough to make statistical comparisons between a large number of securities while automatically varying the start and end dates. Once a correlation is found, its defining characteristics can be studied and used as the basis for additional research. This iterative approach will allow a private investor to continually make unique discoveries that can become true sources of value creation. The programming tools available in today's spreadsheets and databases make this kind of software development relatively straightforward. Excel, for example, includes a robust library of prewritten statistical functions, and most of the programming logic depends on simple loop structures that increment starting and ending dates. Microsoft has taken an additional step by replicating SQL Server data mining functions in Excel. The tools are freely available on Microsoft's SQL Server Web site as a "data mining add-in" for the Office suite. The data mining facility allows nonprogrammers to accomplish complex tasks that uncover hidden relationships and patterns in large datasets.

Figure 1.3 displays the results of a comparative data mining experiment designed to identify triggers for entering and exiting option positions on the Philadelphia Gold/Silver Index (ticker: XAU).[4] The results can also be used to time investments in physical gold. In this context gold is represented by the SPDR Gold Trust exchange traded fund (ticker: GLD).[5] The results are somewhat complex because rather than directly comparing prices or price changes, the chart relates the GLD/XAU ratio to the value of XAU. That is, some time frames are characterized by a precise relationship between the GLD/XAU ratio and the value of XAU.

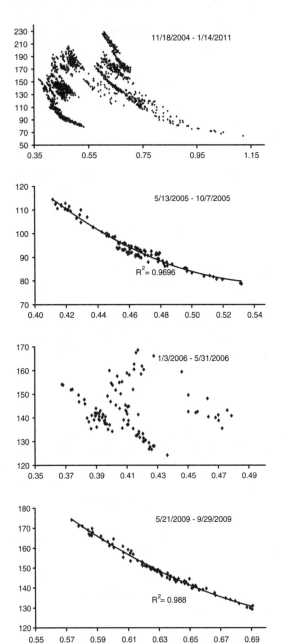

FIGURE 1.3
Relationship between the GLD/XAU ratio and XAU for different time frames. In each case the x-axis measures the GLD/XAU ratio, and the y-axis measures the price of XAU alone. The first chart displays a two-dimensional scatterplot covering approximately 1,500 days from the launch of the GLD ETF in November 2004 until mid-January 2011, when these words were written. The second chart displays a unique time frame during the second half of 2005, when the ratio was highly predictive. The third chart covers the first half of 2006, when the relationship disintegrated. The fourth chart covers a second time frame (May–September 2009) when the GLD/XAU ratio, once again, could be used to predict the price of XAU.

The first chart displays calculated ratios for 1,500 days (nearly 6 years). The starting date was chosen because it represents the launch of the SPDR Gold Shares exchange traded fund. The final date corresponds to the writing of this text. The three charts that follow, therefore, each span time frames that are contained in the first chart. However, the coherent relationship revealed in charts 2 and 4 are impossible to detect in the large amount of noise that dominates the overall pattern.

Such is always the case in data mining experiments. The goal in this case is to discover a set of conditions that signal a stable market and to use the appearance of this signal as an entry point for trading. Investors who follow this type of strategy would remain out of the market most of the time, but when they entered, their trades would have a very high probability of being profitable. In this regard, charts 2 and 4 can be thought of as islands of stability that cannot be readily identified in chart 1.

Excel provides statistical tools that allow such identification. The simplest is the basic r-squared calculation noted in the chart. These charts were created using a 4-column spreadsheet with the price of GLD in column A, XAU in column B, the GLD/XAU ratio in column C, and r-squared in column D. R-squared was calculated using a window of 20 price changes, and extended runs where the value climbed above 0.9 were selected for charts 2 and 4. This simple approach facilitates the rapid identification of a trend without any complex programming.

During the time frame of the second chart (5/2005–10/2005), intraday entry points for option trades could be identified as subtle deviations from the trend line. Intraday values above the line represented high-gold/low-XAU combinations, and points below the line represented low-gold/high-XAU (points displayed in the chart were calculated using closing values for the two ETFs). The time frames were also different with regard to the behavior of gold.

During the volatile time frame of chart 3 (1/2006–5/2006), gold prices were characterized by multiple $50 increases and drawdowns. This high level of volatility created complex financial challenges for the mining companies represented in XAU. These companies normally hedge their business with gold futures, and managing these hedges is difficult when gold prices are unstable. A private investor with access to this information would also have been wise to avoid the gold market while it remained unstable. Option traders, however, have an advantage because they can structure trades that profit from instability and underpriced risk. Traders who pursue this approach would be most active during times that displayed the random fingerprint of chart 3.

Finally as mentioned above, chart 4 (2/2009–9/2009) spans a second coherent time frame when predictability returned to the gold market. Once again, a clear relationship existed between the GLD/XAU ratio and the price of XAU.

Unlike simple statistical analyses, data mining experiments often involve open-ended searches for new correlations. In this example we discovered both the existence of a correlation and two different time frames for which it was valid (5/2005–10/2005 and 5/2009–9/2009). By using variable-length sliding windows and refining the analysis, we can construct a library containing different datasets with valid correlations. Library entries can then be compared with news events and market data to discover the most favorable conditions. The goal is to identify a set of conditions that mark the beginning and end of a correlation time frame.

Focusing on a Statistical Anomaly

Data mining experiments are most helpful when the goal is to discover new statistical correlations. The same databases and query tools can also be used to test theories about market behavior. One interesting example involves the "pinning" effect that causes many stocks to gravitate toward a strike price as options expiration approaches. This effect, which has been the focus of an enormous number of academic research papers, can be exploited by option traders who structure unique positions that take advantage of accelerated time decay near the end of an expiration cycle. The distortion is especially large on expiration Friday, when all remaining time premium is lost during the final 6.5 hours. The consensus is that this behavior is driven by delta hedging of a large number of long positions. Research suggests that the unwinding of these positions on expiration day causes the returns of optionable stocks to be altered by an average of at least 16.5 basis points, which translates into an aggregate market capitalization shift on the order of $9 billion. The effect is most evident in option series that exhibit high levels of open interest. Supporting evidence shows that the pinning effect is not evident in stocks that do not have listed options.

Statistical information can be used to spot targets for pinning effect trades. The most obvious questions relate to the behavior of individual stocks: Which are most affected and how often do they expire within specific distances of a strike price? The first step involves collecting and analyzing expiration-day data for an extended period of time for a large number of stocks. Once the behavior of the group is broadly understood, individual stocks can be chosen for more detailed analysis.

Unfortunately, the problem is complex because stocks that "pin" to a strike price on expiration day often drift away near the close as traders close their positions. A better measure is the number of minutes containing a strike price cross. A simple data mining experiment might involve a first-pass identification of stocks that close near a strike price followed by a more detailed minute-by-minute analysis of specific stocks that tend to exhibit strike price effects.

Table 1.1 contains information about the expiration-day behavior of 328 optionable stocks over $50, as well as a select group of 17 stocks that rank near the top of the list with regard to their likelihood of closing near a strike price on expiration day. The table compares the number of closings within $0.50 of a strike price during the 12 monthly expirations of 2010 with the number of such events on a random day (10 days before expiration was chosen as the random day). The first row of the table reveals that the broad group of 328 stocks generated 818 close proximity closings over the 12 expirations but only 758 such events on the 12 random days—an 8% increase on expiration day. The list of 328 stocks was sorted according to the difference between the number of expiration and nonexpiration events and the top candidates were selected. Each of the members of the list closed expiration within $0.50 of a strike at least 5 times during the 12 months and exhibited at least 4 additional close proximity events across the 12 expirations measured. Results are listed in the table. ESRX (Express Scripts) tops the list. It closed within $0.50 of a strike price 7 of 12 months but only once on the random day.

TABLE 1.1 *Expiration and nonexpiration closing behavior for optionable stocks over $50. Row 1 reveals the difference for the broad group; row 2, the select group. Individual members of the select group are listed in rows 4–20.*

	Expiration Day	Exp – 10 Days
328 stocks	818	758
Select stocks	91	16
ESRX	7	1
AGCO	6	1
BUCY	6	1
CF	6	1
EMN	6	1
GOOG	6	1
BCR	4	0
CNX	5	1
DECK	5	1
FLS	6	2
LZ	4	0
MAN	5	1
MLM	4	0
MON	4	0
PM	6	2
POT	6	2
VNO	5	1

The next step in the analysis involves studying minute-by-minute expiration-day behavior for individual candidates on the list. Most of today's trading platforms contain data at the individual minute level along with an export function that allows the data to be uploaded to a spreadsheet. TradeStation was used to construct an example using ESRX. A worksheet was created that included every minute of the 2010 trading year: 4,674 expiration-day minutes and 93,181 non-expiration-day minutes. (TradeStation contains a function that can be used to flag expiration-day minutes.) A simple Excel statement can be used to identify the nearest strike for each row of the spreadsheet. If, for example, the stock is trading in a range that has $5 spacing, the statement would be this:

```
Strike = (Round(CurrentClose / 5)) * 5
```

This simple operation divides the closing price by 5, rounds the result to the nearest integer, and multiplies by 5 to recover the nearest strike. An Excel conditional can then be used to determine whether an individual minute contains a high above the strike and a low below. If column D3 contains the minute high, E3 the low, and H3 the strike, the following statement would set a flag in the form of a "1" if the minute contained a strike cross:

```
=IF(AND(D3>=H3,E3<=H3),1,0)
```

The statement can be written once at the top of a new column and replicated for all records using cut and paste. Once a column of flags are set, the sum will reveal the number of minutes containing a strike cross. This approach was used to tally up the number of expiration and nonexpiration minutes that contained strike crosses for ESRX. The results revealed that 1% of nonexpiration minutes crossed a strike while the probability on expiration day was 3.7%. The analysis included a total of 97,855 minutes.

Minutes that close within a preselected distance of a strike price can also be identified. For example, the statement if(Abs(close-strike)<0.1,1) can be used to flag each record with a close less than 10 cents from the nearest strike by placing a "1" in the cell containing the conditional. As before, the column is summed to determine the number of minutes meeting this criterion. For daily data, this approach reveals the number of days closing within a predetermined distance of a strike.

This information can be used by stock and option traders to structure statistically advantaged positions that have a high probability of delivering a profit on expiration day. Minute-by-minute data can be used to discover other subtle distortions that can provide trading advantages. For example, the worksheet can be sorted to reveal whether the largest single-minute price changes tend to occur at a particular time of day. The approach that was actually taken involved creating an Excel macro that sequentially tested various closing distances from the nearest strike price, tabulated the total number of strike crosses, calculated the true range of each minute in terms of (high-low)/low, and generated a variety of statistical measures of trend-following behavior. Several worksheets were created and macros were used to sort the data and generate summary tables. In Chapter 3, "Advanced Topics," we will construct a detailed example that includes these principles and approaches along with conditional statements, Boolean logic, and sample VBA code.

Stocks that exhibit the pinning effect often experience large price spikes near the close when most large positions have been unwound. We would likely exploit this phenomenon by trading long straddles in the final few hours. The most promising candidates would be stocks that consistently exhibit a tendency toward large price changes on expiration Friday. Our analysis would be based on the percent change from high to low and would use an extended version of the software that we used to study the pinning effect. The results are surprising—19 stocks exhibited expiration-day price changes averaging 5% or more. We would further analyze each long straddle candidate by comparing expiration and nonexpiration price-change behavior, and by assessing the fairness of implied volatility for the option contracts. After narrowing the field to a small number of stocks, we would review minute-by-minute expiration-day charts to look for specific triggers. Key parameters would include time, volume, and relationship to the price changes of the broad market.

The steps involved in creating Table 1.1 are straightforward but certainly not trivial. Some programming skills are required. Open, high, low, and closing prices, along with volume and date information for all optionable stocks over $50, were downloaded into an Excel spreadsheet. The complete dataset for 383 stocks and 12 months consisted of approximately 83,000 records—a trivial number for modern spreadsheets. A date arithmetic macro was used to identify expiration-day records. Simply stated, the macro used Excel's weekday function to identify Friday records, and flagged those that occurred between days 15 and 21 of each month (equity and index options expire on the Saturday following the third Friday of each month). The dataset was further reduced by sorting and removing expiration-day records with closing prices below $49.50. This step was necessary because many stocks with December 2010 closing prices above $50 traded significantly lower during previous expiration cycles. Removing these records made sense because our goal was to study the behavior of stocks in the over-$50 price range. We chose $49.50 as a cutoff so that closing events that were 50 cents below the $50 strike price would be included. The final dataset contained around 4,000 expiration-day records for 383 stocks. New stocks that did not span the entire 12 expiration cycles were also excluded.

Many different data management strategies are possible, and in some cases they are necessary. For example, Excel had a capacity limit of only 65,536 rows prior to the release of Office 2007. A simple solution for large datasets involved downloading the raw data to an Access or SQL Server database and running the same date arithmetic macro mentioned previously. Expiration Friday records were then exported from the database to an Excel spreadsheet, where sorting and tabulating operations were performed on the reduced dataset. This solution is generally preferable since it allows very large datasets to be analyzed without regard to the capacity of the spreadsheet. It also takes advantage of performance characteristics of databases that are optimized for handling hundreds of thousands or millions of records. In this case the database already contained a table of expiration dates that was used to identify expiration Fridays in the large dataset. A simple SQL query was used to capture the overlap between the tables:

```
SELECT *
FROM Over50, ExpirationDates
WHERE (Over50.day = ExpirationDates.day)
```

Over50 was the name of the table that contained pricing information for optionable stocks greater than $50 (380,000 records spanning 2 years). Expiration Dates was the name given to the relatively small table that contained a list of expiration Fridays. Each table had a date field called day—thus the line WHERE (Over50.day = ExpirationDates.day). Surprisingly, all 380,000 records can be processed on a typical personal computer in just a couple of seconds. The output consisted of the 18,600-record subset that was exported to Excel for final analysis. Solutions that use both databases and spreadsheets are a central theme of this book. Generally speaking, spreadsheets are not efficient databases, and databases are poor spreadsheets, even though some of their capabilities overlap.

Throughout this book, we will return to more detailed discussions of database and spreadsheet structures, associated macros, relevant statistical functions, and the logistics that underlie such projects. However, in its simplest form the expiration-day example will serve to illustrate some important concepts. First and foremost is the value of general-purpose solutions that are built around standard languages and reusable data structures. The database infrastructure that we created for this example contains a reusable table of expiration dates and a general-purpose template for storing historical stock data. We can manipulate new data added to the structure with simple queries written in SQL—a standard tool available with all databases. As we saw, simple SQL queries are very efficient and they facilitate the processing of large amounts of data. Over time we can assemble a library of simple queries that can be easily modified to execute virtually any database search task. We can also add more complex programs that accomplish tasks beyond the limits of a simple SQL query. An example would be the automated creation of a table containing multiple sliding-window volatility calculations across a large population of stocks. We could, for example, decide to calculate the daily volatility for 1,000 different stocks across a 2-year time frame using windows of 20 days (1 month), 90 days (1 quarter), and 252 days (1 trading year). We could also add other statistical calculations—kurtosis and skewness—and automatically generate a summary table containing the number of spikes greater than 1, 2, 3, and 4 standard deviations for each stock measured against one of the windows. The database would become a repository of information that could be extended with new data after the market close each day. Figure 1.1 was generated from such a database using the 20-day volatility window for OIH. A simple SQL query extracted the data, which was then exported to Excel, where the figure was created. The operation required only a minute or so of time because the necessary database infrastructure was already in place.

Using standard query tools and a general-purpose database also ensures that the system is extensible—that is, we can add new data sources and programs as they are needed. Had we constructed our system around a single vendor's proprietary database and/or programming language, we would have lost this flexibility. Such a system can only be extended with a very limited number of compatible data sources, and programs can only be written in a particular vendor's proprietary programming language. Several of today's most popular data vendors offer simplified scripting languages that can be used to compare and test trading strategies. While their similarity to spoken languages makes them relatively simple to learn, the power and flexibility of these tools is severely limited. Moreover, the programs that are developed are usually interpreted at runtime, meaning that the script is not precompiled into fast machine-readable object code. As a result, large programs written in these proprietary scripting languages are often quite slow. Conversely, contemporary general-purpose languages like C++, Java, and Visual Basic offer the flexibility to create complex programs that connect to a variety of data sources while benefiting from the performance of a compiler. Program steps are translated into machine-readable object code before the program is run and, in most cases, the compiler is sophisticated enough to handle embedded command sequences written in SQL.

The system we are discussing is an infrastructure consisting of two distinct classes of tools. The first includes the sort of commercially available charting and data analysis software that has become familiar to millions of investors. Online brokers and data vendors often create packages of these tools as differentiators of their services. Typical components include real-time charting software and data feeds that contain equity and option prices, a package of indicators with appropriate back-testing facilities, access to news wires with a system of filters and alerts, customizable option pricing screens that include the Greeks, and methods for setting triggers and alerts. Most packages also include a scripting language that can be used to back-test trading strategies. Option traders tend to use these tools throughout the trading day.

This book focuses on the second class of tools—data infrastructure and management software. These are the databases, spreadsheets, and associated programs that are used to analyze historical prices and other information. Large investment banks and brokerages spend millions of dollars each year developing these systems, which, through their algorithmic trading capabilities, have become the drivers of most of the volume on the world's exchanges. They have also become core components in virtually every large-scale risk management strategy. The result has been a rapid evolution from risk management scenarios based on simple hedging to more complex risk arbitrage solutions. In today's financial markets risk is distributed more than it is hedged.

The flexibility to retrieve answers to a variety of complex historical questions is central to risk management. Consider, for example, a portfolio manager attempting to structure a hedge to protect against a 5% market correction (up or down). Relevant historical data might include the frequency of such events during the past several years, implied volatility of the market just before each event, value of the CBOE Volatility

Index (VIX) before and after each event, and the relative differences between close-to-close and high-to-low changes. Table 1.2 displays this data for all price changes that exceed 5% for the S&P 500 index between January 1990 and the end of December 2007. The data reveals that close-to-close changes tend to understate intraday activity as measured by high-to-low transitions. As expected, the VIX tends to rise in a drawdown and fall when the market rises. Surprisingly, there is no correlation between the VIX, which measures volatility priced into equity options, and actual implied volatility of the index. Before 2008, price changes this large were very rare—there were only 10 in the 4,538 trading days represented in the chart (0.2%). Moreover, the September 2001 attacks did not trigger a price change large enough to be included despite a lengthy market closure that had the potential to disrupt underlying price-discovery mechanisms.

TABLE 1.2   *All high-low price changes greater than 5% for the S&P 500 index (January 1990–November 2007). The gray bar marks the first trading day after the September 2001 attacks. This record is included even though it did not meet the 5% criterion.*

Date	Open	High	Low	Close	Close Change	Close Chng %	H-L Chng %	Volat	VIX Before	VIX After
19971027	941.64	941.64	876.73	876.98	-64.66	-6.87%	6.89%	0.29	23.17	31.12
19971028	876.99	923.09	855.27	921.25	44.27	5.05%	7.35%	0.35	31.12	31.22
19980831	1027.14	1033.47	957.28	957.28	-69.86	-6.80%	7.37%	0.34	39.60	44.28
19980901	957.30	1000.71	939.98	994.26	36.98	3.86%	6.07%	0.36	44.28	36.48
19981015	1005.53	1053.15	1000.12	1047.49	41.96	4.17%	5.04%	0.31	38.96	33.34
20000404	1510.05	1526.22	1417.22	1494.73	-11.24	-0.75%	7.14%	0.25	24.03	27.12
20000414	1436.67	1436.67	1339.40	1357.31	-83.20	-5.78%	6.77%	0.28	29.40	33.49
20010103	1279.75	1347.76	1274.62	1347.56	64.29	5.01%	5.43%	0.33	29.99	26.60
20010917	1090.23	1090.23	1037.46	1038.77	-53.77	-4.92%	4.84%	0.24	31.84	41.76
20010919	1032.74	1038.91	984.62	1016.10	-16.64	-1.61%	5.23%	0.24	38.87	40.56
20020724	794.11	844.32	775.68	843.43	45.73	5.73%	8.13%	0.39	44.92	39.86

The rarity of these events makes them difficult and expensive to persistently hedge. It is this observation that has led institutional investors to alter their risk management strategies. The events also appear to be clustered—two in 1997, three in 1998, two in 2000, two in 2001, and one in 2002. Only 5 of 18 years are involved. However, the market has changed substantially in the past few years. If we extend this analysis to include 2008–2010, the number of events climbs from 11, as listed in Table 1.2, to 64. The final 2 years include nearly five times as many large high-low intraday transitions as the previous 18 years.

Table 1.3 accommodates this distortion by listing high-low transitions larger than 8% over the entire 20-year time frame. Of the 14 events listed, 13 occurred after 2008. Despite these extreme circumstances, options implied volatility remains relatively low. When these words were written in January 2011, the VIX was a surprisingly low 15.4 and true historical volatility of the S&P 500 measured in a 20-day window was even lower at 6.3%. This discrepancy alone is cause for concern because, as we shall see, the ratio between real and implied volatility is often more important than the absolute values.

TABLE 1.3   *All high-low price changes greater than 8% for the S&P 500 index (January 1990–December 2010).*

Date	Open	High	Low	Close	Close Change	Close Chng %	H-L Chng %	Volat	VIX Before	VIX After
20020724	794.11	844.32	775.68	843.43	45.73	5.6%	8.1%	0.39	50.48	45.29
20080929	1209.07	1209.07	1106.39	1106.39	-106.62	-9.2%	9.3%	0.52	34.74	46.72
20081006	1097.56	1097.56	1007.97	1056.89	-42.34	-3.9%	8.5%	0.58	45.14	52.05
20081009	988.42	1005.25	909.19	909.92	-75.02	-7.9%	10.6%	0.63	57.53	63.92
20081010	902.31	936.36	839.80	899.22	-10.70	-1.2%	10.7%	0.63	63.92	69.95
20081013	912.75	1006.93	912.75	1003.35	104.13	11.0%	9.4%	0.76	69.95	54.99
20081015	994.60	994.60	903.99	907.84	-90.17	-9.5%	10.0%	0.80	55.13	69.25
20081016	909.53	947.71	865.83	946.43	38.59	4.2%	8.7%	0.80	69.25	67.61
20081022	951.67	951.67	875.81	896.78	-58.27	-6.3%	8.5%	0.82	53.11	69.65
20081028	848.92	940.51	845.27	940.51	91.59	10.2%	10.1%	0.85	80.06	66.96
20081113	853.13	913.01	818.69	911.29	58.99	6.7%	10.4%	0.70	66.46	59.83
20081120	805.87	820.52	747.78	752.44	-54.14	-6.9%	9.7%	0.72	74.26	80.86
20081201	888.61	888.61	815.69	816.21	-80.03	-9.4%	8.9%	0.76	55.28	80.51
20100506	1164.38	1167.58	1065.79	1128.15	-37.72	-3.3%	9.0%	0.21	24.91	32.80

Extending the analysis through the end of 2010 revealed distinct tendencies for significant price-change events to cluster. This tendency also manifests itself at lower price-change levels and can be used as a confirmation of rising volatility. The behavior often signals the end of a significant rally or strong sustained uptrend. Had we extended the time frame of our original analysis to the beginning of 1985, the clustering effect would have become much more apparent than it was during the relatively calm years of Table 1.2.

The extended time frame includes 14 additional events, 11 of which occurred in 1987—the year of the famous 25% crash. Table 1.4 lists each of the 1987 events in chronological order.

TABLE 1.4   All high-low price changes greater than 5% for the S&P 500 index during 1987.

Date	Open	High	Low	Close	Close Change	Close Chng %	H-L Chng %	Volat	VIX Before	VIX After
19870427	281.52	294.45	276.22	281.93	0.41	0.15%	6.19%	0.24	30.23	31.46
19871016	298.08	298.92	281.52	282.70	-15.38	-5.16%	5.82%	0.29	27.86	36.37
19871019	282.70	282.70	224.83	224.84	-57.86	-20.47%	20.47%	0.85	36.37	150.19
19871020	224.84	245.62	216.46	236.83	11.99	5.33%	11.87%	0.87	150.19	140.00
19871021	236.83	259.26	236.83	258.38	21.55	9.10%	8.65%	0.94	140.00	73.91
19871022	258.38	258.38	242.99	248.25	-10.13	-3.92%	5.96%	0.94	73.91	102.22
19871026	248.22	248.22	227.26	227.67	-20.55	-8.28%	8.44%	0.97	98.81	113.33
19871028	233.19	238.58	226.29	233.28	0.09	0.04%	5.15%	0.98	97.51	81.24
19871029	233.28	246.69	233.28	244.77	11.49	4.93%	5.44%	1.00	81.24	64.66
19871103	255.75	255.75	242.78	250.82	-4.93	-1.93%	5.07%	1.02	54.90	58.44
19871130	240.34	240.34	225.78	230.30	-10.04	-4.18%	6.06%	0.29	42.11	46.13

The April event (top line) was characterized by a very large intraday move greater than 6% that was not mirrored in the close-to-close price change. The post-April time frame that ended with the October drawdown was characterized by rising volatility and close-to-close price changes that more closely mirrored intraday changes. Figure 1.4 displays historical volatility for the S&P 500 during this time frame. Data points for the chart were calculated using a 20-day sliding window.

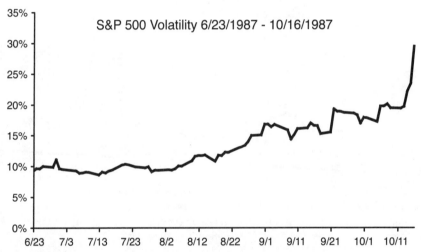

FIGURE 1.4 *S&P 500 historical volatility 6/23/1987–10/16/1987 (calculated using a 20-day sliding window). Volatility is displayed on the y-axis, dates on the x-axis.*

Rising volatility as measured by close-to-close price changes was one of many indications that risk was increasing. Many investors who took additional queues from events that unfolded in fixed-income and currency markets made the decision to short the equities markets or purchase out-of-the-money puts. They were rewarded in October when the broad market declined 25%. During this time frame, both historical and options implied volatility climbed to more than 100%. The market began to stabilize in November and by year-end the S&P 500 was back above its January opening value. Figure 1.5 maps historical volatility (dark line) of the S&P 500 against the value of the index (light line) for the entire year.

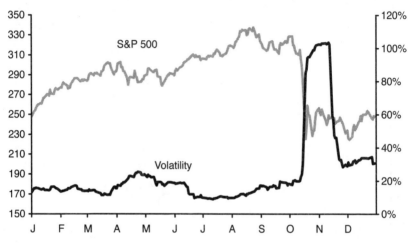

FIGURE 1.5   *S&P 500 index (gray line) and historical volatility (dark line) for the 1987 trading year. Volatility was calculated using a 20-day sliding window. S&P 500 closing values are displayed on the left y-axis, volatility on the right y-axis, and the beginning of each month on the x-axis.*

The first volatility increase around day 78 marks a drawdown of nearly 7% that included the April event listed in Table 1.3. The market subsequently stabilized, with volatility falling to historic lows, before following the path outlined in Figure 1.4. A similar pattern of alternating corrections and rallies marked by rising and falling volatility was evident in the market crash of 1929. As in 1987, the market became unstable and volatility climbed steeply between early summer and late

October. The trend is evident in Figure 1.6, which displays the volatility of the market calculated, as before, using a 20-day sliding window.

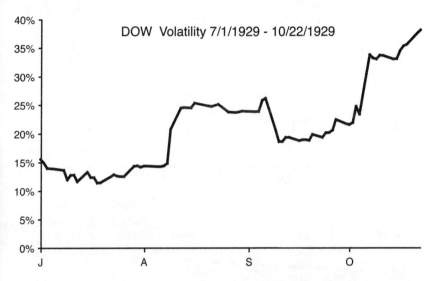

FIGURE 1.6 *Dow historical volatility 7/1/1929–10/22/1929 (calculated using a 20-day sliding window). Dow volatility is displayed on the y-axis, months on the x-axis.*

Although the 1929 precrash volatility increase is slightly steeper and more erratic than that of the 1987 crash, the dynamics are similar. The corresponding full-year profile is displayed in Figure 1.7.

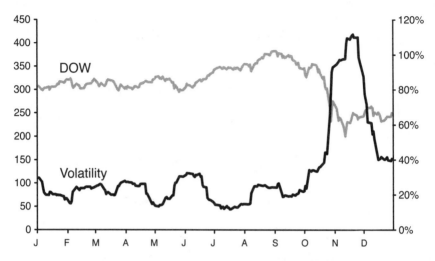

FIGURE 1.7   *Dow (gray line) and historical volatility (dark line) for the 1929 trading year. Volatility was calculated using a 20-day sliding window. Values for the Dow are measured on the left y-axis, volatility on the right y-axis. The beginning of each month is marked on the x-axis.*

Both charts reveal a significant late rally that preceded the crash, and in both cases market volatility climbed during the rally. This trend should be considered disturbing because market volatility usually falls during a rally. Generally speaking, rising volatility is considered to be a sign that risk is increasing, and falling (or low) volatility is considered to be bullish. This interpretation of market behavior has been anchored by the closely followed CBOE Volatility index (VIX). Professional investors are often alarmed when the VIX rises during a rally. However, the VIX measures implied volatility priced into options on S&P 500 stocks, not historical (realized) market volatility. The difference can be significant because the VIX has a tendency to instantly respond to news and market changes, whereas realized volatility calculations must necessarily span some time frame. The answer is to construct a picture of the market by observing realized volatility that is calculated using windows of varying length, in addition to the VIX and other volatility indicators. The CBOE also provides several different measures including an indicator that measures the market's expectation of future volatility over a 3-month time frame (VXV), and an arbitrage indicator (VTY) that reveals the difference between implied and realized market volatility. The first can be used in combination with the VIX to track changes in the S&P volatility term structure, whereas the latter measures variance between the VIX and realized volatility of the index.[6] As always, the goal is to build the most comprehensive market view and to find structures that correlate with specific types of behavior.

Before structuring a risk management strategy, it would be wise to repeat the analysis using different price-change thresholds and time frames. A complete analysis would include all declines between 1% and 10% in time frames as brief as a single day and as long as a month. It would also make sense to compare different indexes. Risk management is a never-ending process because, despite appearances, the amount of historical data is quite limited. We have very few crashes to compare, the number of significant drawdowns is limited, and changing market conditions complicate the comparison. The past can be a poor indicator of the future.

Data visualization tools are a critical component of any data management strategy because they make it possible to quickly view and analyze large amounts of information.

Sometimes a simple mathematical operation accompanied by a new display format can provide new insights into a dataset. Figure 1.8 provides an example. The top chart displays 200 days of closing prices for Apple Computer. The bottom chart contains the same information transformed to display each price change in standard deviations measured against the most recent 20-day volatility window. In this context each closing price is recast as an up or down spike measured against the standard deviation of the previous 20 daily returns—a daily return is calculated as log(close #2/close #1).[7] We will return to a detailed discussion of price-change behavior and the price-spike charting format in the next chapter.

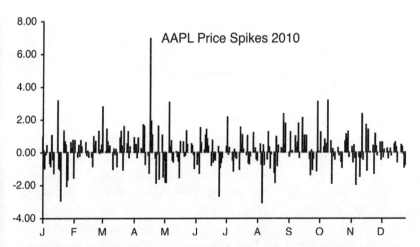

FIGURE 1.8   *Upper chart reveals 1 year of closing prices for Apple computer. Lower chart contains the transformed data which expresses each close as a
price spike calculated in standard deviations measured against the most recent
20-day volatility window. Both charts mark the beginning of each month on
the x-axis. The large upward price spike visible in the April time frame immediately followed the first-quarter-earnings release on April 21.*

Despite their dramatically different appearances, the two charts contain the exact same data in the same sequence. Following are the steps used to calculate each price spike displayed in the second chart:

1. Calculate and store the log of each price change.

2. Calculate the standard deviation of 20 price changes (21 days).

3. Multiply the result of step 2 by the closing price on day 21 to determine the magnitude of a 1 standard deviation price change in dollars.

4. Calculate the day 22 price change (day 22 close - day 21 close).

5. Divide the day 22 price change by the value of a 1 standard deviation change determined in step 3.

6. Roll the 20-day window forward 1 day and repeat the calculation.

It is difficult to overstate the value of data visualization tools because they often provide insights that cannot be obtained in any other way. While the upper chart of Figure 1.8 does not provide much meaningful information, the lower chart allows us to visually quantify the stock's price-change behavior across an extended time frame. The figure reveals a distinct difference between the size and frequency of upward and downward spikes. This information is helpful to an option trader because these differences generate option price distortions. In this example upward price changes of 3 and 4 standard deviations are common while downward spikes rarely exceed 2 standard deviations. Implied volatility of calls would need to rise 20% above put volatility to erase the distortion.

Such pricing discrepancies cannot persist because they create arbitrage opportunities that rapidly unwind. From a statistical perspective, calls were consistently underpriced in this example and puts were overpriced. Certain structures such as call-back spreads consistently generate profit in these scenarios. The discrepancy is significant because the requirement for put-call parity prevents its disappearance. We will explore other visualization methods that can help option and stock traders identify new investment opportunities. These methods are most often used in conjunction with data mining strategies that are designed to uncover new mathematical relationships.

In this regard, the power and relative simplicity of today's development tools has leveled the playing field by making it possible for private investors to create their own databases and related software infrastructure. The cost of computing power has also declined dramatically with multi-gigahertz multicore CPU desktop computers becoming commonplace. Some investors are even constructing their own Linux clusters and realizing the benefits of high-performance parallel computing. Projects that once required a software development team can now be accomplished by an individual with limited programming skills, and enormous databases can fit on a desktop computer. These capabilities make it possible for individual investors to attack extremely complex data mining problems. Among the most difficult are those that quantify the links between economic news items and price-change behavior of specific equities. This type of analysis is dependent on a variety of sophisticated algorithms that can extract and classify events from textual data—e.g., news feeds. One of the more difficult underlying tasks involves decorating time series data with various events to create heterogeneous composite information. This heterogeneous data must then be analyzed to discover price-change patterns that are not apparent in the absence of the events. Complex as this might sound, it is well within the reach of any determined investor with a personal computer, a connection to the Internet, and a database.

Many different pieces of relevant economic news are released each week. Each news item represents a potentially important event that can drive both the market and individual stocks. Examples include, but are not limited to, consumer confidence, employment data, supply-chain money flow, business inventories and spending, gross domestic product growth, inflation data, and trade imbalances. Different securities respond to each of these items in different ways. In some cases the news and the market's reaction combine to affect the behavior of an individual security. Such relationships can be discerned with context-sensitive data mining tools. The following functions are central to a software infrastructure that supports complex data mining of textual information.

Event Extraction

Events must be extracted and classified from textual data such as news feeds. One of the most difficult technical challenges involves constructing a data dictionary that can be used to extract specific categories from semistructured data. For example, the category "missed earnings" might not be apparent in the statement "analysts were disappointed today when XYZ corporation reported earnings that were 2 cents below expectation." Other categories are more obvious in their original context—"oil prices rose 2% today"; "the chairman of XYZ stepped down"; "consumer confidence set a new record." Each of these statements includes words that can be classified and stored in a data dictionary.

Context Discovery

Traditional technical analysis is context free; the market is not. If, for example, consumer confidence were to rise unexpectedly, the market might be expected to react positively. However, in an inflationary environment where monetary tightening is having a negative effect on the market, high levels of consumer confidence might be considered to be negative news. Context discovery requires the development of software for parsing and semantically analyzing phrases. Many examples of such software exist in the biomedical world, where researchers routinely search large text databases containing descriptive medical information.

Time Series Correlation

Price changes are captured in the form of a time series, and the effects of specific events are measured as distortions in the series. One strategy is to sort multiple sets of repeating time series into two groups—one that contains a potentially distorting event for each series and one that does not. Neural network and pattern discovery software can then be used to create weighting functions that are capable of distinguishing between the two groups. In this regard it is important that the key event be consistently aligned in each time series.

Data mining experiments that combine price-change information with insights gleaned from textual analysis represent a high level of sophistication. Many variations and combinations are possible. The most advanced examples involve capturing and analyzing news feeds in real time with the goal of executing trades rapidly enough to capitalize on the changes of a fast-moving market. The goal is a reasonable one because even highly efficient markets—those characterized by strong-form efficiency—have winners and losers. It is certainly possible to profit from trends that reliably persist for several minutes, and many event-driven market moves persist for several hours. The objective should be to raise the level of accuracy, not the level of sensitivity. Restated in engineering terms, it is the signal-to-noise ratio that matters most. Data mining approaches that generate a large number of triggers often fail when the probability of being right is just slightly greater than the probability of being wrong. A much better approach is to select stringent conditions that generate a small number of very accurate trade triggers. Many successful investors have developed systems that generate just a few triggers each year that each have a very high probability of success. Option traders can capitalize on this level of accuracy by doubling or tripling their investment in a brief period of time.

Critics of this philosophy will be quick to point out that a strategy that is right 55% of the time should generate a constant positive return across a large number of trades. Unfortunately, this approach does not fully comprehend the realities of trading. An unreliable trigger must be managed with very sensitive stop orders that limit profit even when the trigger works. Reducing the sensitivity of stop orders allows wider price fluctuations that are beneficial when a trade is moving in the profitable direction. However, the increased tolerance to price fluctuations also causes larger losses when the market moves against a trade. Bid-ask spreads further complicate the situation. If we eliminate stop orders altogether, we are making the assumption that positive and negative moves have the same magnitude, and that our 55/45 advantage will generate a profit simply because we are right more often than wrong. Generally speaking, it is very difficult to profit from a small statistical advantage.

Capitalizing on Rare Events

Sometimes it is possible to predict unusual events with a very high level of certainty. If the magnitude is large enough, the results can be enormously profitable. The most obvious candidate is a sharp market correction. Investors who were properly invested in short stock, short index, or out-of-the-money long put positions during the crashes of 1987, 2000, or 2008 made enormous amounts of money. Smaller corrections in the 10% range also yield tremendous opportunities.

An increasingly popular approach to quantifying market uncertainty involves tracking the difference between actual volatility of the S&P 500 index and implied volatility of S&P options as represented by the VIX. Professional traders have focused on this difference for several years. Their interest stems from the observation that options implied volatility tends to be consistently larger than actual volatility of the market. Not surprisingly, the gap tends to widen when the market becomes unstable.

Activity in this area was strong enough to prompt the CBOE Futures Exchange (CFE) to introduce a product that allows investors to buy or sell the S&P 500's realized volatility over a period of 3 months (CBOE S&P 500 Three-Month Variance Futures were introduced in June 2004). More recently, the CBOE decided to extend this theme with a benchmark that tracks the performance of a hypothetical volatility arbitrage trading strategy that capitalizes on the difference between implied volatility of S&P 500 index options and actual volatility of the index (CBOE S&P 500 VARB-XTM Strategy Benchmark—ticker: VTY).

Evolution of this trend has taken us from simple stock investing, to betting on volatility, to trading the difference between actual volatility and implied volatility of options on the broad market. Although the vast majority of investors will never trade this complex arbitrage, the benchmark along with the VIX and other volatility indexes provides a valuable set of indicators that everyone can learn to use.

Predicting Corrections

Investors who follow the VIX often make the mistake of believing that a relatively low value indicates that the market is stable. Unfortunately, this misconception tends to be compounded by the financial news media. As mentioned in the previous section, the ratio between the VIX and true historical volatility of the market is a more relevant measure of uncertainty. A low ratio signals that market participants are not pricing in additional risk premium; a high ratio is a sign of market uncertainty. In this discussion, we will refer to the ratio as VIX/true.

The importance of the ratio came sharply into focus in early April 2010, when the VIX had fallen as low as 17 but the VIX/true ratio peaked above 2.5. The market fell sharply, correcting 13% in 8 weeks. Stabilization occurred and the correction ended when the ratio fell below 1. Conversely, in February 2009 with the VIX hovering above 50, the market entered into a sustained rally—exactly opposite the expectations of most investors who interpret a high VIX as a signal of instability. During this time frame, however, true volatility remained relatively high, peaking above 40%. These dynamics are apparent in Figure 1.9, which displays both the VIX/true ratio (right y-axis), the S&P 500 (left y-axis), and notes regarding the value of the VIX at key points during this time frame. The upward sloping line that connects peaks in the VIX/true ratio reveals a steadily rising series of peaks that signal the market's increasing reluctance to price risk at levels corresponding to the actual volatility.

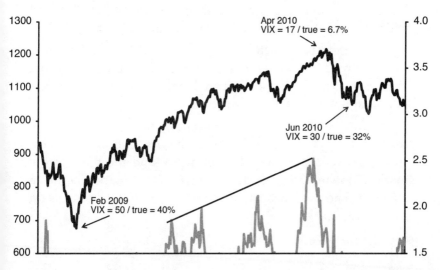

FIGURE 1.9 *S&P 500 declines and advances and the VIX/true ratio. The value of the S&P 500 is marked on the left y-axis; the VIX/true ratio (gray line) is marked on the right y-axis.*

These dynamics have been true for many years. During the 3,000 trading days ending in December 2010, the ratio averaged 1.3—that is, the VIX averaged 1.3X the underlying volatility of the S&P 500 calculated in a 20-day window. Between early 1999 and the end of 2010, the ratio rose sharply four times, peaking above than 2.3. The April–June 2010 correction visible in Figure 1.9 represented one of the four events. In early April the VIX posted a value of 17 while 20-day historical volatility had fallen to just 6.7%.

Three occurrences of a highly distorted VIX were associated with various waves of the NASDAQ collapse. A fourth followed closely after, at the beginning of the recovery in September 2003. Following the fourth distortion, the market experienced four large oscillations over a 9-month time frame. During these oscillations, the S&P climbed as high as 1150 and fell as low as 1060—a volatile time, to say the least.

More important, each large spike in the VIX/true ratio was followed by a reversal in which the ratio ultimately fell below 1. In each case, the low ratio signaled that the market had stabilized and the drawdown was over.

Figure 1.10 illustrates this concept by tracing the S&P 500 through the NASDAQ meltdown. The first two arrows mark spikes above 2.3 in the VIX/true ratio, and the third arrow marks a downward spike that occurred as the market began to stabilize. The chart begins on September 5, 2000, and ends on March 13, 2003.

FIGURE 1.10   *Key points in the VIX/true ratio during the NASDAQ meltdown.*

Brief Time Frames

These dynamics are also valid in the short-term. Figure 1.11 traces implied volatility for Apple $320 puts between 1:00 PM and 3:10 PM on December 13, 2010, when the stock suddenly fell $5 to just below a strike price. The trading price of the stock is displayed on the left y-axis, and implied volatility for the put is measured on the right y-axis. Individual points on the chart are calculated using a 5-minute interval. Implied volatility of the near-the-money put was a perfect leading indicator, rising just before the stock fell.

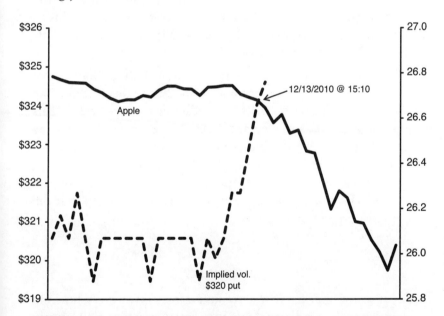

FIGURE 1.11 *Implied volatility of near-the-money options as a leading indicator of a short-term correction. Apple 5-minute closing prices are displayed on the left y-axis and implied volatility for the $320 put on the right y-axis.*

In this regard it is important to choose an option with a high delta that is sensitive to small moves in the underlying stock. In-the-money options, however, can yield misleading results. This phenomenon is related to actual trading behavior. A long investor will often accept a slightly discounted price to close a highly profitable in-the-money trade, whereas a short investor might overpay to quickly close a losing position. These dynamics create noise in the form of rising and falling volatility. Conversely, far out-of-the-money options are relatively insensitive to the behavior of the underlying stock. The example depicted in Figure 1.11 represents an ideal situation because the stock moved from $5 out-of-the-money to just a few cents below the strike. Market participants who were short the $320 put responded urgently when the stock began to fall.

Generally speaking, charts that display implied volatility for near-the-money options are one of the best indicators for day trading. The options market often responds to news and events that have not yet surfaced at the retail investor level by pricing in corrections several minutes before they occur. This behavior is most apparent in heavily traded stocks like Apple for which institutional investors hold option positions involving several strikes. Their behavior represents a level of efficiency that did not exist a few years ago.

Summary

Because the market is a zero sum game, investors who limit themselves to traditional off-the-shelf indicators will always lose money to sophisticated traders armed with more powerful tools. The days of buying and selling stocks when moving averages cross or when an oscillator reaches one side of a channel are over. Moreover, investors who fool themselves into believing that they can exploit some combination of these indicators are making a huge mistake. Times have changed. Today's sophisticated investors tend to focus their attention on analyzing subtle distortions in volatility and identifying anomalies in derivative prices. The popularity of complex products like the VARB-XTM Strategy Benchmark represents a natural evolution of this trend.

Throughout this book, we focus on methods that have the capacity to uncover correlations and reliable trade triggers that are based on anomalies and price distortions. This is not a book on technical charting—there are already dozens of fine texts devoted to that topic. It is also not a book for those who seek a "get rich quick" investing solution. Our goal will be to develop skills and tools that can continue to reveal new trading opportunities without regard to changes in market behavior and the world economy.

Further Reading

Cataldo, A. J., and A. A. Savage, *The January Effect and Other Seasonal Anomalies: A Common Theoretical Framework (Studies in Managerial and Financial Accounting)*, JAI Press, January 2000.

D'Mello, R., S. P. Ferris, and C. Y. Hwang, "The Tax-Loss Selling Hypothesis, Market Liquidity, and Price Pressure Around the Turn-of-the-Year," *Journal of Financial Markets,* vol. 6, no. 1 (January 2003): 73-98.

Fama, E. F., "Market Efficiency, Long-term Returns, and Behavioral Finance," *Journal of Financial Economics,* vol. 49, no. 3 (September 1998): 283-306.

Hansen, P. R., and A. Lunde, "Testing the Significance of Calendar Effects," Brown University Department of Economics Working Paper No. 2003-03 (January 2003).

Haugen, R. A., and J. Lakonishok, *The Incredible January Effect: The Stock Market's Unsolved Mystery*, Dow Jones-Irwin, 1988.

Ni, S. X., N. D. Pearson, and A. M. Poteshmana, "Stock Price Clustering on Option Expiration Dates," *Journal of Financial Economics*, vol. 78, no. 1 (May 2005): 49-87.

Sullivan, R., A. Timmerman, and H. White, "Dangers of Data Mining: The Case of Calendar Effects in Stock Returns," *Journal of Econometrics*, vol. 105, no. 1 (November 2001): 249-286.

Szakmary, A. C., and D. B. Kiefer, "The Disappearing January/Turn of the Year Effect: Evidence from Stock Index Futures and Cash Markets," *Journal of Futures Markets*, vol. 24, no. 8 (August 2004): 755-784.

Endnotes

1. Stocks and options were priced in increments of 1/16 (6.25 cents).

2. Daily Telegraph 9/23/2001.

3. Edwin Maberly and Daniel Waggoner, "Closing the Question on the Continuation of Turn-of-the-month Effects: Evidence from the S&P 500 Index Futures Contract," Federal Reserve Bank of Atlanta working paper 2000-11, August 2000.

4. The Philadelphia Gold/Silver Index (ticker: XAU) is a capitalization-weighted index composed of 16 companies involved in the gold and silver mining industry.

5. Gold can be purchased through the SPDR Gold Trust (ticker: GLD)—an exchange traded fund (ETF) that tracks the price of gold.

6. Term structure measures the effect of time on implied volatility. It can be visualized in a plot of implied volatility for at-the-money options versus expiration month.

7. Multiplying the standard deviation of the daily returns by the square root of the number of trading days per year gives the annual volatility.

Chapter 2

The Basics

Spreadsheet Versus Database

Both databases and spreadsheets are critical components in a software infrastructure that is designed to manage large amounts of financial history information. Databases serve as information repositories because they can store many years of data for thousands of securities. A well-designed system contains many tables that are linked together and indexed to form a complete structure containing a variety of financial metrics for both individual securities and markets. Databases have a tendency to grow over time as more information is acquired. For example, a price-history database might be extended with large amounts of text data extracted from news wires. This additional data would be stored separately from the price-change information that it is designed to complement but could be accessed using custom queries that take advantage of links between the tables. These constructs and their implied capacity requirements drive the requirement for a database.

While databases are the most efficient vehicles for storing and processing large diverse datasets, spreadsheets are undeniably the best choice for managing a single table of numerical information. Until recently, spreadsheets suffered from significant capacity limitations. Just a few years ago it would have been impossible, for example, to export a database table containing 200,000 records to a spreadsheet for further analysis. Those limitations vanished when Microsoft released Excel 2007. The maximum number of rows increased from 65,536 to 1,048,576, and the column limit was raised from 256 to 16,384. As a result, it is now possible to import a database table containing more than 1 million records and any conceivable number of fields. The increased capacity makes Excel an excellent complement to a large database infrastructure.

The enormous capacity of Excel that began with the 2007 version can sometimes blur the distinction between spreadsheets and databases. Suppose, for example, that we decided to create a single table containing daily open, high, low, close, and volume information for 1,000 stocks across 3 years. Our table would contain 756,000 rows and 7 columns (Symbol, Date, Open, High, Low, Close, Volume). Pre-2007 spreadsheets could only handle tables that were less than 10% this size. The answer was to download all records into a single database table and to export portions of the table into Excel as needed. Today, however, it is entirely reasonable to build a single worksheet containing this many records. As a result, systems have become more balanced and decisions about moving data between spreadsheets and databases are based on function rather than capacity. Building on this theme, Microsoft has included a set of functions designed to help manage data in a range of cells that are designated as a database. Excel 2010 raised the bar even higher with full 64-bit support. Rather than being a theoretical limit, million-row spreadsheets have become reasonable solutions to many technical problems that formerly could only be handled in databases.

In this chapter we will focus on a variety of calculations and numerical transformations that are well suited to spreadsheets. Due to Excel's broad array of mathematical functions, many of these operations can be completed without any programming. It is often possible to construct a complex statement that compresses several different functions and calculations into a single cell, and to copy and paste that cell thousands of times with just a few mouse clicks. We will also review graphical methods that can be used to identify trends and patterns in financial data. These capabilities can complement those of traditional charting software to provide insights that ultimately form the basis of new trading strategies.

Managing Date Formats

Excel has become the de facto standard in spreadsheets partly because of its ability to integrate disparate data sources. Using Excel's Import Wizard, we can capture historical prices and dates from a variety of sources as either text or numbers. Once the information is contained in a spreadsheet, it can be transformed into many different formats. No special handling is required for numbers because the *General* format of Excel will recognize both numbers and text. Highlighting the column and selecting a more specific cell format such as *Number - Decimal places:* 2 is a convenient way to standardize the representation of a column, but it is generally not necessary. Other choices include *Percentage, Currency, Fraction,* and *Scientific*

Notation. Regardless of the format selected, Excel will properly store and recognize numbers that are originally imported from other sources as text. Mathematical operations performed on these numbers will yield correct answers and their format can be changed at any time.

Dates are more complex than numbers. Although Excel recognizes a variety of date formats, conversions from text—normally accomplished using the DATEVALUE function—can be cumbersome depending on the source. Some sources require no conversion at all. For example, Yahoo! Finance displays historical stock prices in tables that use the dd-mmm-yy format. Using this format, September 23, 2007, would be represented as 23-Sep-07. Excel automatically recognizes these values as dates. A straightforward method for converting unrecognized text-based date strings involves creating a new string using the year, month, and day portions of the original, and converting the new string into an Excel date via the DATE function. Year, month, and day portions can be extracted with the LEFT, MID, and RIGHT text-management functions.[1] Suppose, for example, that our data source exports dates in the yyyy-mm-dd format—that is, each entry consists of a 4-digit year, 2-digit month, and 2-digit day concatenated into a single string. Suppose, for example, that the text to be converted is stored in cell A1 as 20070923 (September 23, 2007). Individual components of the date string can be extracted as outlined here:

Year (2007):   LEFT(A1,4)

Month (09):   MID(A1,5,2)

Day (23):   RIGHT(A1,2)

Using these components and Excel's DATE function, we can assemble a single string that will provide the system with a properly formatted date:

```
DATE(LEFT(A1,4), MID(A1,5,2), RIGHT(A1,2))
```

Properly formatted dates support date arithmetic in the sense that they can be added, subtracted, and included in other calculations. Excel stores dates as sequential numbers, also referred to as serial numbers. In Windows systems the default starting date, serial number 1, is January 1, 1900. The default starting date for Macintosh systems is January 2, 1904. However, Windows and Macintosh versions each support both date systems—only the default settings are different.[2] The contents of a cell recognized by the system as a date can be displayed in several different formats. Assuming we are using a Windows-based system, the result in our example can be displayed as Sunday, September 23, 2007, 23-Sep-07, 2007/09/23, or the serial number 39348.

Calculating option prices often involves more precision than can be achieved using closing prices and "days until expiration." Monthly equity and index options expire on the Saturday following the third Friday of each month at 5:00 p.m.; the number of days remaining before expiration becomes an increasingly inaccurate measure as the final trading day of each expiration cycle approaches. On the final day at 9:30 a.m., option contracts actually have 31.5 hours (1.3125 days) left before expiration. At 4:00 p.m., when the stock market closes, they have 25 hours left (1.04167 days). The resulting price distortion can be significant, especially for at-the-money options. To compensate for this problem, many option pricing programs are designed to calculate the number of minutes left before expiration. Excel is an excellent platform for writing programs that calculate Black-Scholes values because it includes a set of time functions that can be used to generate precise calculations. Complete date entries can be formatted as yyyymmdd h:mm—that is, a 4-digit year, 2-digit month, 2-digit day, 1-2 digit hour, and 2-digit minute. As with simple dates, these entries can be added, subtracted, and included in other calculations. Extending our previous example, September 23, 2007, 6:00 a.m. would take on the serial value 39348.2500. We can view the serial number simply by changing the format of the cell to *General* or *Number* (when selecting *Number,* specify 4 decimal places).

Finally, because Excel cannot be expected to properly interpret the century of a 2-digit year, it is advisable to always use the 4-digit format. If only 2 digits are used, they will be interpreted as follows:

00 through 29 is interpreted as 2000 through 2029.
"29/12/23" will be recognized as December 23, 2029.

30 through 99 is interpreted as 1930 through 1999.
"30/12/23" will be recognized as December 23, 1930.

The example given near the beginning of this section (23-Sep-07) would yield an incorrect date if "07" was intended to mean 1907. It is easy to imagine how failing to fully specify a year with all 4 digits can result in confusing errors. Such errors are very difficult to track down when they occur in macros or Visual Basic programs because the problem relates to a subtlety of convention rather than a programming mistake.

We will return to date and time arithmetic in various contexts throughout this book because time decay is a core component of every option contract price. Precision becomes increasingly important as expiration day approaches and day-of-week information can be a key component of historical price analysis. Our database discussion will include a description of a calendar reference table, we will explore the use of decimal dates that accurately depict spacing in price-history charts, and date arithmetic will be central to our discussion of modeling tools.

Aligning Records by Date

When a worksheet contains multiple ticker symbols, it is often necessary to verify that each contains records for the same dates. Simply verifying the number of records is insufficient because two lists that are the same length can contain different records. A simple test can be accomplished by summing the dates for each ticker and displaying the results as a serial number. Table 2.1 contains a brief example using 10 records for 2 tickers.

TABLE 2.1   *Record consistency verification using a date checksum.*

Symbol	Date	Open	High	Low	Close	Volume
ABC	2007/11/26	112.80	113.38	107.55	107.77	34181
ABC	2007/11/23	111.96	114.11	110.40	112.58	13563
ABC	2007/11/20	114.95	115.24	109.26	111.85	45417
ABC	2007/11/19	120.25	120.63	114.20	114.20	35979
ABC	2007/11/16	120.18	120.98	117.45	118.59	33750
ABC	2007/11/15	125.58	126.91	120.31	120.71	38717
ABC	2007/11/14	124.51	126.58	122.66	125.98	24994
ABC	2007/11/12	120.75	125.72	120.04	122.66	29939
ABC	2007/11/09	132.88	134.30	131.54	131.54	34011
ABC	2007/11/08	136.30	137.77	132.15	134.79	28207
	394,022					
XYZ	2007/11/26	127.52	130.56	125.02	130.28	28541
XYZ	2007/11/23	126.97	129.24	126.50	127.20	21121
XYZ	2007/11/21	126.29	128.39	126.28	126.97	17845
XYZ	2007/11/20	125.63	126.55	124.65	126.15	21809
XYZ	2007/11/19	126.36	126.55	123.39	124.27	43838
XYZ	2007/11/15	133.61	134.83	131.32	131.32	26722
XYZ	2007/11/14	134.78	135.91	131.80	133.18	16854
XYZ	2007/11/13	137.49	139.20	133.77	134.88	18517
XYZ	2007/11/12	137.75	138.92	135.57	136.19	13252
XYZ	2007/11/08	140.49	140.49	135.38	135.85	37276
	394,031					

Each symbol is missing 2 records. The ABC series is missing 11/21 and 11/13; the XYZ series lacks 11/16 and 11/09. Despite having the same number of records, they generate different date checksums (shown in bold). These lists are short and it is fairly easy to spot the missing dates. When the lists contain hundreds of records, an automated approach makes much more sense. We can search for mismatched records using conditional statements. Table 2.2 displays the results of a series of comparisons using Excel's IF function.

TABLE 2.2   *Date alignments are flagged using conditionals of the form* IF(ABC_Date = _XYZ_Date, "" , 1). *Results are shown in the* Test *column.*

Symbol	Date	Close	Symbol	Date	Close	Test
ABC	2007/11/26	107.77	XYZ	2007/11/26	130.28	
ABC	2007/11/23	112.58	XYZ	2007/11/23	127.20	
ABC	2007/11/20	111.85	XYZ	2007/11/21	126.97	1
ABC	2007/11/19	114.20	XYZ	2007/11/20	126.15	1
ABC	2007/11/16	118.59	XYZ	2007/11/19	124.27	1
ABC	2007/11/15	120.71	XYZ	2007/11/15	131.32	
ABC	2007/11/14	125.98	XYZ	2007/11/14	133.18	
ABC	2007/11/12	122.66	XYZ	2007/11/13	134.88	1
ABC	2007/11/09	131.54	XYZ	2007/11/12	136.19	1
ABC	2007/11/08	134.79	XYZ	2007/11/08	135.85	

Each row contains a conditional statement of the form `IF(ABC_Date = XYZ_Date, "",1)`. (`ABC_Date` and `XYZ_Date` are replaced with row and column designations in the actual spreadsheet.) As written, the conditional generates a null character (`""`) in rows where the dates match and the number 1 in rows where the dates are different. The statement can be written once at the top of a column and pasted into all the remaining cells. However, if we adjust the spacing of an individual record, all conditional statements that follow will contain incorrect pointers. For example, inserting a space below the second record of ABC in Table 2.2 would correctly align the dates 2007/11/20 while corrupting the conditional statement so that the record following the new space (ABC record 3) will continue to be compared to XYZ record 3. Conversely, if we made the adjustment by deleting XYZ record 3 (2007/11/21), then the conditional for XYZ record 3 would give an error message because the record it points to no longer exists, and all conditionals that follow would be corrupted.

The solution to this problem is to point to individual records using indirection, which allows a cell to store a pointer to another cell. If, for example, cell M2 contains the value G11, then the statement `INDIRECT(M2)` will return the contents of cell G11. We can use this construct to build a table of pointers that does not suffer from the problem outlined previously. Table 2.3 is designed using this type of indirection.

TABLE 2.3 Date alignments are flagged using conditionals that reference matching pairs of records through indirection. Rows and columns are marked along the edges of the table.

	A	B	C	D	E	F	G	H	I
1	Symbol	Date	Close	Symbol	Date	Close	Ind_1	Ind_2	Test
2	ABC	2007/11/26	107.77	XYZ	2007/11/26	130.28	B2	E2	1
3	ABC	2007/11/23	112.58	XYZ	2007/11/23	127.20	B3	E3	1
4	ABC	2007/11/20	111.85	XYZ	2007/11/21	126.97	B4	E4	
5	ABC	2007/11/19	114.20	XYZ	2007/11/20	126.15	B5	E5	
6	ABC	2007/11/16	118.59	XYZ	2007/11/19	124.27	B6	E6	
7	ABC	2007/11/15	120.71	XYZ	2007/11/15	131.32	B7	E7	1
8	ABC	2007/11/14	125.98	XYZ	2007/11/14	133.18	B9	E8	1
9	ABC	2007/11/12	122.66	XYZ	2007/11/13	134.88	B9	E9	
10	ABC	2007/11/09	131.54	XYZ	2007/11/12	136.19	B10	E10	
11	ABC	2007/11/08	134.79	XYZ	2007/11/08	135.85	B11	E11	1

Columns G and H contain pointers to cells that contain dates. The conditional statements of column I refer to dates using the INDIRECT function and these pointers. Insertions and deletions across columns A through F do not affect these pointers. For example, the test contained in I2 (first record) uses indirection to compare the dates stored in B2 and E2. Inserting or deleting records will not affect the comparison because the formula retrieves its pointers from cells G2 and H2, which always point to dates stored in B2 and E2. Had we pointed to the dates themselves, Excel would have adjusted the references in the formula when insertions or deletions physically moved the records.

The conditional statement used for the comparison becomes most clear when constructed in sections. First we must define the rules for a successful match. It is obvious that a match occurs when ABC_Date and XYZ_Date are equal. Using the test from row 2 as an example, the first comparison is between the dates represented by INDIRECT(G2) and INDIRECT(H2). Our test will be for INDIRECT(G2)=INDIRECT(H2). We must also consider an inserted blank record as a match for its counterpart on the same line, that is, INDIRECT(G2)=0 or INDIRECT(H2)=0. A logical OR is used to combine all three tests: OR(INDIRECT(G2)=0,INDIRECT(H2)=0,INDIRECT(G2)=INDIRECT(H2)). The final statement is wrapped in an IF conditional that generates a 1 if true and a null value if false: IF(OR(INDIRECT(G2)=0,INDIRECT(H2)=0,INDIRECT(G2)=INDIRECT(H2)),1,""). Table 2.3 includes 5 matches. Our goal is to achieve a perfect match across all records including inserted blanks. Table 2.4 displays final results that achieve this goal.

TABLE 2.4 Correctly aligned records for 2 tickers.

	A	B	C	D	E	F	G	H	I
1	Symbol	Date	Close	Symbol	Date	Close	Ind_1	Ind_2	Test
2	ABC	2007/11/26	107.77	XYZ	2007/11/26	130.28	B2	E2	1
3	ABC	2007/11/23	112.58	XYZ	2007/11/23	127.20	B3	E3	1
4				XYZ	2007/11/21	126.97	B4	E4	1
5	ABC	2007/11/20	111.85	XYZ	2007/11/20	126.15	B5	E5	1
6	ABC	2007/11/19	114.20	XYZ	2007/11/19	124.27	B6	E6	1
7	ABC	2007/11/16	118.59				B7	E7	1
8	ABC	2007/11/15	120.71	XYZ	2007/11/15	131.32	B8	E8	1
9	ABC	2007/11/14	125.98	XYZ	2007/11/14	133.18	B9	E9	1
10				XYZ	2007/11/13	134.88	B10	E10	1
11	ABC	2007/11/12	122.66	XYZ	2007/11/12	136.19	B11	E11	1
12	ABC	2007/11/09	131.54				B12	E12	1
13	ABC	2007/11/08	134.79	XYZ	2007/11/08	135.85	B13	E13	1

We achieved a perfect alignment by inserting blank records where dates were missing. However, an equally valid method would involve deleting dates that were not present in both ticker lists. If many symbols are being processed, it is often best to begin the sheet with a master date list that is used as a reference across the entire worksheet. The master list is most often assembled from a ticker that is known to contain the full complement of records.

Large alignment problems can easily contain hundreds or even thousands of rows. The solution is to create a Visual Basic program that automates the logical steps described previously. An example is displayed in Listing 2.1.

LISTING 2.1   *Excel VBA program for aligning records by date.*

```
 1: Sub AlignRecords()
 2: Dim Row As Long
 3: Dim LeftCell As String
 4: Dim RightCell As String
 5: Dim RangeString As String

 6: Row = 2
 7: While (Cells(Row, "B") <> "") And (Cells(Row, "E") <> "")
 8: If Cells(Row, "B") > Cells(Row, "E") Then
 9:   LeftCell = "D" & Row
10:   RightCell = "F" & Row
11:   RangeString = LeftCell & ":" & RightCell
12:   Range(RangeString).Select
13:   Selection.Insert Shift:=xlDown, _
      CopyOrigin:=xlFormatFromLeftOrAbove

14: Else
15:   If Cells(Row, "E") > Cells(Row, "B") Then
16:     LeftCell = "A" & Row
17:     RightCell = "C" & Row
18:     RangeString = LeftCell & ":" & RightCell
```

```
19:    Range(RangeString).Select
20:    Selection.Insert Shift:=xlDown, _
       CopyOrigin:=xlFormatFromLeftOrAbove
21:  End If
22: End If
23: Row = Row + 1
24: Wend
25: End Sub
```

The program assumes the same construct as Tables 2.3 and 2.4. Records for the first ticker appear in columns A–C; second ticker records occupy columns D–F. In each case the order is Symbol, Date, Close. In line 6 we initialize with Row=2 because the first row is assumed to contain column labels. The logic is contained within a single While...Wend loop (lines 7–24) that continues until one of the columns is blank and there are no more comparisons to be made:

```
While (Cells(Row, "B") <> "") And (Cells(Row, "E") <> "")  ³
```

As in Tables 2.3 and 2.4, the date order is assumed to be descending. In rows where the date corresponding to the first ticker (column B) is greater than the second (column E), blank cells are inserted in columns D–F. The process is reversed if the second ticker contains a higher date value. Cells are inserted using Excel's Range.Insert method, which inserts a range of cells and shifts others away to create space. The direction of the shift is apparent in the program statements on lines 13 and 20:

```
Selection.Insert Shift:=xlDown, _
CopyOrigin:=xlFormatFromLeftOrAbove
```

Running this program using the data from Table 2.3 would generate the results displayed in Table 2.4. Columns G, H, and I are extraneous and will not be read by the program. Using this code, tens of thousands of records can be processed in just a few seconds on a typical desktop computer.

Two important options are missing: an automatic accommodation for the date order, ascending or descending, and the ability to delete blank spaces that correspond to missing records like those contained in rows 4, 7, 10, and 12 of Table 2.4. The simplest most flexible solution to the latter involves creating a second program, which is displayed in Listing 2.2.

LISTING 2.2 *Excel VBA program for removing unmatched records after date alignment.*

```
 1: Sub RemoveSpaces()
 2: Dim Row As Long
 3: Dim TestRow As Long
 4: Dim LeftCell As String
 5: Dim RightCell As String
 6: Dim RangeString As String

 7: Row = 1
 8: While Cells(Row, "B") <> "" Or Cells(Row, "E") <> ""
 9:   Row = Row + 1
10: Wend

11: For TestRow = Row To 1 Step -1
12:   If Cells(TestRow, "B") = "" Or Cells(TestRow, "E") = "" Then
13:     LeftCell = "A" & TestRow
14:     RightCell = "F" & TestRow
15:     RangeString = LeftCell & ":" & RightCell
16:     Range(RangeString).Select
17:     Selection.Delete Shift:=xlUp
18:   End If
19: Next TestRow
20: End Sub
```

As in the first program, the logic is relatively straightforward. The program first scans through the table searching for the bottom, then reverses direction, checking each row and deleting those that contain a blank record. By deleting from the bottom of the table, we avoid the complex logic that accompanies deleting more than one record on a single line as cells are shifted up. It is never necessary to effect more than one deletion on a single row if the direction of movement is from bottom to top. The reverse was true in the first program where blank records were inserted and the most expedient solution involved migrating from the top to the bottom of the worksheet. The reader is encouraged to verify this logic either with a spreadsheet or with pencil and paper.

The test in line 8 uses an Or conditional to ensure that the program has advanced past the last record for both tickers. This construct is necessary because inserting blank records creates misalignments that can cause one ticker to exceed the other by many rows. The For...Next loop contained in lines 11–19 reverses direction, backing up from the bottom of the table and deleting rows that contain a blank record. Excel's Range.Delete method, used in line 17, removes the blanks. The program, which is very brief, can be written in only a few minutes. By combining both programs, we can quickly align two datasets and delete days that do not contain a record for each.

As always, there are many ways to accomplish the same task. For example, we could have used Excel's SpecialCells method to identify the last cell in the worksheet and capture a value for the final row. Lines 7–10 would be replaced with the following code:

```
Dim Last as Range
Set Last = Range("A1").SpecialCells(xlLastCell)
    Row = Last.Row
```

Although this method is more efficient, it has some draw-backs. If a dataset with more rows appears somewhere else in the worksheet, Last.Row will return an inappropriately large number. The program will effectively be tricked into deleting a large number of blank rows well beyond the end of the records contained in columns A–F. Additionally, because Excel remembers the largest range until the worksheet is saved, deleting a large dataset without saving the file can generate confusing results. This example is one of many in which the method we choose is the best compromise between simplicity and efficiency.

As mentioned previously, we can easily add a feature that automatically accommodates either ascending or descending dates. Listing 2.3 contains the code for a program that has been extended with both features; that is, it uses the logic of Listing 2.2 to remove blank records, and it automatically accommodates both ascending and descending dates.

LISTING 2.3 *Excel VBA record alignment program with extensions for handling ascending and descending dates and deletion of unmatched records.*

```
 1: Sub AlignRecordsComplete()
 2: Dim Row As Long
 3: Dim TestRow As Long
 4: Dim Direction As Integer
 5: Dim LeftCell As String
 6: Dim RightCell As String
 7: Dim RangeString As String

 8: If Cells(2, "B") > Cells(3, "B") Then
 9:   Direction = 1
10: Else: Direction = 2
11: End If

12: Row = 2
13: While (Cells(Row, "B") <> "") And (Cells(Row, "E") <> "")
```

```
14:  Select Case Direction
15:  Case 1
16:  If Cells(Row, "B") > Cells(Row, "E") Then
17:    LeftCell = "D" & Row
18:    RightCell = "F" & Row
19:    RangeString = LeftCell & ":" & RightCell
20:    Range(RangeString).Select
21:    Selection.Insert Shift:=xlDown, _
       CopyOrigin:=xlFormatFromLeftOrAbove

22:  Else
23:    If Cells(Row, "E") > Cells(Row, "B") Then
24:      LeftCell = "A" & Row
25:      RightCell = "C" & Row
26:      RangeString = LeftCell & ":" & RightCell
27:      Range(RangeString).Select
28:      Selection.Insert Shift:=xlDown, _
         CopyOrigin:=xlFormatFromLeftOrAbove
29:    End If
30:  End If

31:  Case 2
32:  If Cells(Row, "B") < Cells(Row, "E") Then
33:    LeftCell = "D" & Row
34:    RightCell = "F" & Row
35:    RangeString = LeftCell & ":" & RightCell
36:    Range(RangeString).Select
37:    Selection.Insert Shift:=xlDown, _
       CopyOrigin:=xlFormatFromLeftOrAbove

38:  Else
39:    If Cells(Row, "E") < Cells(Row, "B") Then
40:      LeftCell = "A" & Row
41:      RightCell = "C" & Row
42:      RangeString = LeftCell & ":" & RightCell
43:      Range(RangeString).Select
44:      Selection.Insert Shift:=xlDown, _
         CopyOrigin:=xlFormatFromLeftOrAbove
```

```
45:    End If
46:   End If
47:   End Select
48: Row = Row + 1
49: Wend

50: While Cells(Row, "B") <> "" Or Cells(Row, "E") <> ""
51:   Row = Row + 1
52: Wend

53: For TestRow = Row To 1 Step -1
54:   If Cells(TestRow, "B") = "" Or Cells(TestRow, "E") = "" Then
55:     LeftCell = "A" & TestRow
56:     RightCell = "F" & TestRow
57:     RangeString = LeftCell & ":" & RightCell
58:     Range(RangeString).Select
59:     Selection.Delete Shift:=xlUp
60:   End If
61: Next TestRow
62: End Sub
```

Although this version of the program is considerably longer, the number of variables remains small. The additional length results from repetition of the logic for identifying and correcting date mismatches. The descending date logic of lines 15–30 is repeated for the ascending date case in lines 31–46. The only change required is a reversal of the > sign used in the tests contained in lines 16 and 23. In the descending date case we correct a mismatch by inserting blank cells and shift the remaining records down in the column with the smaller date. The ascending date case requires the opposite: Records are shifted down in the column with the larger date. Lines 8–11 compare successive dates at the beginning of the file to determine the proper direction. The result of that comparison is used to set a flag in the variable Direction (lines 9, 10). The flag is interpreted by the program's Select Case statement in line 14, and the correct set of instructions is subsequently executed—lines 15–30 for the descending case or lines 31–46 for the ascending case. The logic for removing blank records is copied from Listing 2.2 into lines 50–61 of the current program.

These programs are significant because they reveal the capabilities that can be made available with a small amount of programming. Microsoft VBA is relatively easy to learn. Dozens of books on the subject are available; online help is well organized and thorough; Microsoft, through its developer Web site, provides technical papers on key topics; and the Macro Recorder can be used to generate code fragments that can be directly embedded in larger programs. The latter can be of great assistance to anyone seeking to learn the programming steps for a specific task. For example, the code for setting a range and inserting blank cells can be generated by turning on the Macro Recorder, manually inserting the cells using the mouse, and then stopping the recorder. The resulting Visual Basic program will consist of just a few steps that can be cut and pasted into a larger program. Once the correct syntax is known, the details can be appropriately altered. This approach was used to generate the code for inserting and shifting cells in the previous example. The Macro Recorder was used to generate a small program that inserted cells in a specific location. The code was then modified to insert cells at a location pointed to by the variable RangeString. Additional lines of programming were added that create a new RangeString variable for each iteration of the program. This approach can be used to generate code for any task that can be manually executed.

We could continue to modify and extend our program to accomplish a variety of tasks. One useful addition might be a feature that increments the column pointer and begins processing a new dataset each time the program reaches completion.

In this way a large number of individual tickers can be arrayed across the worksheet from left to right. One approach is to compare each new dataset to a reference column, and to continue removing unmatched records from both sides until all tickers and the reference contain the exact same dates. This approach requires two passes through the data. The first pass reduces the reference to a list that contains only records that are present in all other tickers; the second pass further reduces the contents of each ticker to match the final version of the reference. Suppose, for example, that the reference includes dates A, B, C, D, E; ticker #1 includes dates A, B, C, D; and ticker #2 includes dates B, C. The first comparison with ticker #1 removes E from the reference, leaving A, B, C, D. It is then compared to ticker #2 and A, D is removed—only B and C remain. However, ticker #1 still contains records corresponding to A, B, C, D (the records that remained after initial comparison to the reference). Records A and D are removed from ticker #1 during the second comparison to the reference. A third pass is not required.

The new code requires other modifications that are related to the adjustable column pointer. Most significant is the addition of a function that converts a column number to a letter designation. Although Excel generally recognizes that column "E" is the same as column "5," the Range.Insert method does not accept numeric designations. Therefore, each time the column pointer is incremented, the new value must be converted to its string equivalent. The conversion is not trivial because it must include 2-letter designations for values greater than 26, that is, "AA" and beyond. Before each iteration, the program must also check to make sure that the end of the dataset has not been reached. Listing 2.4 contains the enhanced program and a function for converting column numbers to letter designations. The data format is assumed to be the same as before, with each ticker occupying 3 columns (Symbol, Date, Price). The reference occupies columns A–C; ticker #1, D–F; ticker #2, G–I; and so forth. As before, the program is designed to handle either ascending or descending dates.

LISTING 2.4   *Excel VBA record alignment program for multiple tickers.*

```
 1: Sub AlignMultipleTickers()
 2: Dim SymCol As Integer
 3: Dim DateCol As Integer
 4: Dim CloseCol As Integer

 5: Dim Sym_Col As String
 6: Dim Date_Col As String
 7: Dim Close_Col As String

 8: Dim Iterations As Integer
 9: Dim Row As Long
10: Dim TestRow As Long
11: Dim Direction As Integer
12: Dim LeftCell As String
13: Dim RightCell As String
14: Dim RangeString As String

'determine date direction
15: If Cells(2, "B") > Cells(3, "B") Then
16:   Direction = 1
17: Else: Direction = 2
18: End If

19: For Iterations = 1 To 2
20:   SymCol = 4
21:   DateCol = 5
22:   CloseCol = 6

'exit when blank column is encountered
23: While Cells(2, SymCol) <> ""
```

```
24:  Sym_Col = ColumnLetter(SymCol)
25:  Date_Col = ColumnLetter(DateCol)
26:  Close_Col = ColumnLetter(CloseCol)

27:  Row = 2
28: While (Cells(Row, "B") <> "") And (Cells(Row, Date_Col) <> "")

29: Select Case Direction
30: Case 1   'decreasing date order
31: If Cells(Row, "B") > Cells(Row, Date_Col) Then
32:   LeftCell = Sym_Col & Row
33:   RightCell = Close_Col & Row
34:   RangeString = LeftCell & ":" & RightCell
35:   Range(RangeString).Select
36:   Selection.Insert Shift:=xlDown, _
     CopyOrigin:=xlFormatFromLeftOrAbove

37: Else
38:   If Cells(Row, Date_Col) > Cells(Row, "B") Then
39:     LeftCell = "A" & Row
40:     RightCell = "C" & Row
41:     RangeString = LeftCell & ":" & RightCell
42:     Range(RangeString).Select
43:     Selection.Insert Shift:=xlDown, _
     CopyOrigin:=xlFormatFromLeftOrAbove
44:   End If
45: End If

46: Case 2      'increasing date order
47: If Cells(Row, "B") < Cells(Row, Date_Col) Then
48:   LeftCell = Sym_Col & Row
49:   RightCell = Close_Col & Row
50:   RangeString = LeftCell & ":" & RightCell
51:   Range(RangeString).Select
52:   Selection.Insert Shift:=xlDown, _
     CopyOrigin:=xlFormatFromLeftOrAbove
```

```
53: Else
54: If Cells(Row, Date_Col) < Cells(Row, "B") Then
55:   LeftCell = "A" & Row
56:   RightCell = "C" & Row
57:   RangeString = LeftCell & ":" & RightCell
58:   Range(RangeString).Select
59:   Selection.Insert Shift:=xlDown, _
      CopyOrigin:=xlFormatFromLeftOrAbove
60: End If
61: End If
62: End Select

63: Row = Row + 1
64: Wend

'continue to last record then back up and delete blanks
65: While Cells(Row, "B") <> "" Or Cells(Row, Date_Col) <> ""
66: Row = Row + 1
67: Wend

68: For TestRow = Row To 1 Step -1
69: If Cells(TestRow, "B") = "" Or Cells(TestRow, Date_Col) = "" Then
70:   LeftCell = "A" & TestRow
71:   RightCell = "C" & TestRow
72:   RangeString = LeftCell & ":" & RightCell
73:   Range(RangeString).Select
74:   Selection.Delete Shift:=xlUp

75:   LeftCell = Sym_Col & TestRow
76:   RightCell = Close_Col & TestRow
77:   RangeString = LeftCell & ":" & RightCell
78:   Range(RangeString).Select
79:   Selection.Delete Shift:=xlUp
80: End If
81: Next TestRow
```

```
'move to next ticker
82: SymCol = SymCol + 3
83: DateCol = DateCol + 3
84: CloseCol = CloseCol + 3
85: Wend

86: Next Iterations '2nd pass through all tickers
87: End Sub

88: Function ColumnLetter(ColumnNumber As Integer) As String
89:   If ColumnNumber > 26 Then
90:     ColumnLetter = Chr(Int((ColumnNumber - 1) / 26) + 64) & _
        Chr(((ColumnNumber - 1) Mod 26) + 65)
91:   Else:  ColumnLetter = Chr(ColumnNumber + 64)
92:   End If

93:End Function
```

The list of declarations is expanded to include pointers to the 3 columns that contain symbol, date, and price information for each ticker. A new variable is also added to count the 2 passes (iterations) that must be completed. The new function (ColumnLetter) occupies lines 87–93 beyond the end of the main program. It uses a sequence of numerical operations to map numbers to characters for columns from A to ZZ. If necessary, the function can be extended to accommodate the full range of Excel 2007/2010—columns A through XFD.

Each pass through the data is initiated in lines 19–22, where the symbol, date, and closing price columns are reset to 4, 5, 6 (columns D, E, F). The lines that follow (23–26) initiate a second loop that moves the column pointer from left to right. The loop terminates when a blank symbol row is encountered and the pointer is reset for another iteration. Before proceeding, the ColumnNumber function is called to generate string values for each row pointer (lines 24–26). In lines 82–84, after each ticker-to-reference comparison is completed, the 3 column pointers are incremented to align with the next ticker. String equivalents of column values are used throughout the program for consistency. In most instances numeric values would have been properly interpreted by Excel. Line 23 is the exception. We use the numeric value in this instance because the string equivalent has not yet been calculated.

Current and previous versions also differ in the logic for removing misaligned records (lines 68–81). In the previous version we were concerned with only 2 tickers (columns A–F). Before removing a record, we simply set the range to include the current row and all 6 columns. The current version, however, must be able to delete 3 cells from the reference and 3 cells from a ticker at a distant location. The solution involves selecting 2 different ranges and executing separate deletions (lines 74 and 79).

This version of the program represents the endpoint of the present discussion. We began this section by comparing the sums of 2 columns containing date serial numbers. We then progressed to using conditional statements to flag individual mismatches. Indirection was added so that each conditional would continue to point to the same row after records were manually aligned using additions and deletions. Our next step involved automating these processes with Visual Basic programs. We began with a limited example that aligned 2 sets of records with descending dates, and progressed to a relatively complex program that aligns many tickers, deletes unaligned records, and automatically accommodates either date order. With a little practice such programs can be constructed in just a couple of hours.

We could have structured the final program to process vertically oriented files where tickers follow each other in succession and each row comprises a particular date for a single ticker. Logically speaking, each successive row would contain either the next record for the current ticker or the first record of the next. As before, our program would be designed to compare the records for each ticker to a reference, and the final processed file would be a consistent dataset where all tickers contained the exact same dates. This vertically oriented structure more closely resembles a traditional database. It is also extensible in the sense that new columns containing additional or reformatted data can be added without affecting the underlying structure. Each new column represents another field in the database.

In this regard spreadsheets and databases are closely linked. It is relatively easy to paste a spreadsheet directly into Microsoft Access as a database table, and to take advantage of the data management capabilities of the database. Most significant is the ability to form a logical data infrastructure composed of many different tables containing related information. The tables are linked and indexed so that they appear as a single source of information despite being physically distinct entities. We could, for example, construct a database that links historical financial news items with equity prices. The underlying index structure would be designed to link news items to specific tickers, and applications could be written to make the underlying structure transparent. It is also possible to link together a variety of external sources such as Web sites, spreadsheets, and other databases. All of these items can be made to appear as a single source, and the information can be shared among a large number of users. The worksheet we are constructing should be considered a building block for a larger data infrastructure.

In the sections that follow we will build on this approach to construct tables that contain various calculated values for each row. The most obvious candidates are components for traditional charting strategies—moving averages and descriptive ratios using open, high, low, close, and volume information. More subtle candidates include volatility calculations based on windows of varying length and calendar information such as day-of-week, day-of-month, or time remaining before the nearest options expiration. However, before moving on, we will review a key data transformation that is central to the production of proportionally spaced price charts.

Decimal Date Conversion

Traditional stock charting programs display each day's information as if the dates are evenly spaced. They are not. Between Monday and Friday each close occurs 24 hours after the last. However, Friday and Monday closes are spaced by 36 hours. Holidays and weekends represent additional distortions, as do special situations such as the extended market closings that followed the events of September 11, 2001, in the U.S. Proportionally correct stock charts can be created using the sequential serial numbers discussed in the previous section. We can extend this approach by creating more familiar decimal dates that consist of a recognizable year followed by a precisely correct decimal portion of a year. These dates are much easier to understand than the more cryptic serial number format. For example, the Microsoft serial date that corresponds to December 1, 2009, at 4:00 p.m. is 40148.6667. The more comprehensible decimal equivalent is 2009.9169. A quick glance reveals the year 2009 and an additional 91.69% of a year. This number can be generated using Excel's year fraction function (YEARFRAC) along with some additional calculations.

YEARFRAC calculates the fraction of a year represented by the number of whole days between two dates. It uses the syntax

```
YEARFRAC(start_date, end_date, basis)
```

where `basis` defines various calculation methods: 1 for actual/actual, 2 for actual/360, and 4 for actual/365.

The date we want to convert will be represented by `end_date` in the function. The following 3 steps transform `end_date` into a decimal date:

1. Create a string that corresponds to January 1 of the year in `end_date`. This string will represent `start_date` in the year fraction calculation.

2. Use the YEARFRAC function to generate the fraction of a year between the 2 dates.

3. Add the result generated by YEARFRAC to the `start_date` (January 1) to create a decimal date.

We can further adjust the decimal date to represent the 4:00 PM closing time of the market. Since 4:00 PM represents 67% of a single day, the adjustment is equal to $(1/365) \times 0.66667$, or 0.0018. This factor is added to the decimal date to create a final value that will be entered in the table. In the absence of an adjustment, the first day of each year will have a year fraction equal to 0.0000—January 1, 2008, will be represented as 2008.0000. This designation is generally acceptable for most applications. However, attempting to avoid the 0.0000 designation by adding a full day will cause December 31, 2008, to be represented as 2009.0000.

The sequence outlined in Table 2.5 will convert a date (2006/11/20) stored in cell A2 to a decimal date. The conversion uses cell B2 to store the `start_date` (January 1, 2006), cell C2 to store the year fraction, and cell D2 to store the final result including the 4:00 p.m. adjustment.

TABLE 2.5 *Decimal date calculation (3 steps).*

	A	B	C	D
1	Date	DATE(YEAR(A2),"01","01")	YEARFRAC(B2,A2,1)	YEAR(A2)+C2+.0018
2	2006/11/20	2006/01/01	0.8849	2006.8867

The calculation can be copied and pasted across a work-sheet of any length and any number of tickers. It can also be compressed into a single cell:

```
YEARFRAC(DATE(YEAR(A2),"01","01"),A2,1) + YEAR(A2) +0.0018
```

It makes little sense to further automate this process with a program because each line in the table stands alone, crossing between tickers is not an issue, and the entire process can be completed with a single copy-and-paste operation.

Volatility Calculations

Simply stated, we can define volatility as a one standard deviation (StdDev) price change, in percent, at the end of one year. If a stock trades for $100 with a volatility of 30%, then a one standard deviation price change over the span of 1 year will raise the price to $130 or lower the price to $70. Using the normal distribution, we can assume a 68% chance that the final price will fall within this range.

Option pricing models assume that returns are normally distributed and future prices are log-normally distributed. The distinction is important. A normal distribution is symmetrical—for every possible upward price movement there must be a possibility of an equally large downward price movement. Clearly this cannot be possible since a $20 stock can rise to $50 but can never fall to -$10. Suppose, however, that price changes were continuously compounded. Five 10% upward price changes would raise a $20 stock by $12.21 to $32.21. The corresponding downward price changes would reduce the price by $8.19 to $11.81. The continuously compounded upward change is 61%, while the corresponding downward change is only -46%. The distribution of final prices is skewed with the result that no price ever falls below zero. Continuous compounding of normally distributed price changes causes the prices at maturity to be log-normally distributed.

Assuming continuous compounding, it can be shown that volatility is proportional to the square root of time. A 1 standard deviation price change for any time frame is given by the following formula, where ß is the annual volatility and Δt is the percentage of a year:

$$\sigma\sqrt{\Delta t}$$

Using this relationship, we can calculate the size of a 1-week (.0192 year), 1 standard deviation price change for a $100 stock with 30% annual volatility:

$$.30 \times \sqrt{.0192} = .0416$$
$$.0416 \times \$100 = \$4.16$$

There has been much debate over the length of a trading year and the number that should be used for volatility calculations. Although a calendar year is 365 days long, there are actually only 252 trading days. To the extent that volatility calculations are based on daily closing prices, it would seem that 252 is an appropriate number. However, Black-Scholes price calculations are more granular in the sense that they use the number of minutes remaining until options expiration. These calculations are specifically intended to take into account all the remaining time, including weekends. The difference becomes increasingly significant as expiration approaches— the final weekend of the cycle represents 2 of the 7 remaining days. Forward modeling should, therefore, be based on total time remaining, calculated in minutes, as a percentage of a year. Different volatility values can be used and the results compared when determining the fair value of an option contract. An investor might, for example, calculate volatility using different-length windows—20 days to represent the past month and 90 days to measure an entire quarter—in addition to annualization factors based on 252 and 365 days. Each result would generate a different option price when plugged into Black-Scholes or other pricing models.

To calculate historical volatility, we must compute the standard deviation of the short-term returns. The following steps outline the process:

1. Select a standard time frame (1 day, 1 week, 1 month, etc.). Determine the number of time frames per year. The number of time frames is designated (tf) in the formulas below.

2. Compute the return from the beginning to the end of each time frame. If the closing price on day 1 is C_1 and the closing price on day 2 is C_2, then each close-to-close return (R) is given by

$$R = \ln (C_2 / C_1)$$

3. Compute the average value of the returns R_1, R_2, R_3, ...,R_n. If we use 21 closing prices, we will have 20 returns (the value of N in the following formula).

$$R_{avg} = \frac{1}{N} (R_1 + R_2 + R_3 + \ldots + R_n)$$

4. Compute the standard deviation using N-1 statistically "unbiased" weighing. If we have 21 closing prices and 20 returns, n=19 in the following formula.

$$\sigma = \sqrt{tf} \ \times \ \sqrt{1/n \ ((R_1 - R_{avg})^2 + (R_2 - R_{avg})^2 + \ldots + (R_N - R_{avg})^2)}$$

In step 4 we annualize our volatility calculation by multiplying the daily standard deviation by the square root of the number of daily close-to-close price changes in one year. For now we will assume 252 close-to-close changes, and our annualization factor will be based on the square root of 252 (15.875).

This process can easily be executed in a spreadsheet and no programming is necessary. For the purpose of this discussion, we will assume the following column designations:

A—Symbol
B—Date
C—Close
D—Log price change
E—Volatility (20-day window)

First we must calculate the natural logarithm of each price change and store the results in column D: `Ln(close_2/close_1)`. Values for column E are calculated using Excel's `STDEV` function and a moving window of predetermined length. For example, to calculate volatility using a window containing 20 price changes, we would determine the standard deviation for records 2–21 (the 1st price change would occur between records #1 and #2, and the 20th change between records #20 and #21). Since column D contains the price-change data, the standard deviation of the first 20 price changes is given by

`STDEV(D2:D21)`

The process is continued by advancing the window in 1-day (1-row) increments. If our dataset contains multiple tickers, we can add a conditional that checks the beginning and end of each window to make sure that a single standard deviation calculation does not overlap different symbols. The simplest approach is to wrap the standard deviation calculation in a statement that compares the first and last tickers of the window. Calculations are not displayed when the tickers do not match. For a 20-price-change window, this approach will yield 20 blank volatility calculations at the beginning of each new ticker. The unified statement is this:

```
IF(A21=A1,STDEV(D2:D21),"")
```

Readers should note that the conditional test used to compare symbols backs up one additional row to ensure that the first price change measured—in this case D1 to D2—does not begin with a previous ticker. As a result, we calculate the standard deviation using price changes stored in cells D2 to D21 while comparing tickers stored in cells A1 and A21 rather than A2 and A21. Finally, we can extend the statement to provide an annualized volatility calculation. For daily price changes and a 252-day trading year the final version is as shown here:

```
IF(A21=A1,STDEV(D2:D21)*15.87 ,"")
```

Table 2.6 contains a sample template for calculating volatility across multiple tickers. Formulas are displayed in place of price change and volatility calculations, and dates are replaced with simple designations—"Day 1," "Day 2," and so on. Each formula can be written once and copied to all cells in the column with a single copy-and-paste operation.

TABLE 2.6   *Volatility calculation template.*

	A	B	C	D	E
1	Ticker	Date	Close	Price Change	Volatility (20-Day Window)
2	AAA	Day 1	86.47		
3	AAA	Day 2	88.60	LN(C3/C2)	
4	AAA	Day 3	90.31	LN(C4/C3)	
22	AAA	Day 21	86.31	LN(C22/C21)	IF(A2=A22,STDEV(D3:D22)*15.87, "")
23	AAA	Day 22	84.76	LN(C23/C22)	IF(A3=A23,STDEV(D4:D23)*15.87, "")
24	BBB	Day 1	121.19		
25	BBB	Day 2	118.40	LN(C25/C24)	
26	BBB	Day 3	121.33	LN(C26/C25)	
44	BBB	Day 21	122.67	LN(C44/C43)	IF(A24=A44,STDEV(D25:D44)*15.87, "")
45	BBB	Day 22	123.64	LN(C45/C44)	IF(A25=A45,STDEV(D26:D45)*15.87, "")

It is relatively easy to alter the conditions to span windows of different lengths. For example, the first 90-price-change window would be calculated as follows:

```
IF(A2 =A92,STDEV(D3:D92)*15.87,"")
```

We could also employ various calendar arithmetic strategies to generate a table that contains weekly or monthly records and appropriately alter the annualization factor. If, for example, we kept only 1 record per week, our annualization factor would change from 15.87 to 7.21.

Windows that are shorter than a single 24-hour close-to-close time frame should not be overlooked as they can reveal subtle differences between daily and intraday volatility. Virtually all charting packages provide a tool that displays the daily high-low as a percentage of the closing price. Many variations are available; most use a sliding window to average the calculation over some period of time. More sophisticated calculations use weighted averages to emphasize the most recent changes. However, these methods fall short because our principal concern is that intraday volatility could be substantially different than the close-to-close volatility that underlies option contract prices. More specifically, we should be concerned when high levels of intraday volatility result in large price swings that are not comprehended in option prices. We therefore need a method for accurately comparing intraday and traditional close-to-close volatilities.

We can calculate intraday volatility in much the same way that we calculate daily volatility. Since the trading day is 6.5 hours long, the time frame in question is approximately 1/4 the length of a normal close-close cycle—that is, there are 3.7 × 252 such time frames in a trading year (932.4). Appropriate adjustments include replacing close-close price changes with intraday high-low, and using an annualization factor of SQRT(932.4). These upgrades are represented in Table 2.7.

TABLE 2.7 *Intraday volatility calculation template.*

	A	B	C	D	E	F
1	Ticker	Date	High	Low	Price Change	Intraday Volatility (20-Day Window)
2	AAA	Day 1	87.00	85.20	LN(C2/D2)	
3	AAA	Day 2	88.60	87.11	LN(C3/D3)	
4	AAA	Day 3	90.75	87.85	LN(C4/D4)	
21	AAA	Day 20	88.00	84.59	LN(C21/D21)	IF(A2=A21,STDEV(D2:D21)*30.5,"")
22	AAA	Day 21	86.68	83.62	LN(C22/D22)	IF(A3=A22,STDEV(D3:D22)*30.5,"")
23	AAA	Day 22	86.67	84.74	LN(C23/D23)	IF(A4=A23,STDEV(D4:D23)*30.5,"")
24	BBB	Day 1	122.17	119.54	LN(C24/D24)	
25	BBB	Day 2	121.19	118.29	LN(C25/D25)	
26	BBB	Day 3	121.73	117.90	LN(C26/D26)	
43	BBB	Day 20	121.73	117.90	LN(C43/D43)	IF(A24=A43,STDEV(D24:D43)*30.5,"")
44	BBB	Day 21	122.69	120.50	LN(C44/D44)	IF(A25=A44,STDEV(D25:D44)*30.5,"")
45	BBB	Day 22	124.05	121.95	LN(C45/D45)	IF(A26=A45,STDEV(D26:D45)*30.5,"")

Because each row contains its own price change, only 20 rows are required for a 20-day window versus 21 for the close-close calculation. This difference is apparent in Table 2.7 column F, where 23 rows yield 23 volatility calculations. Comparing the two results can yield significant clues to the behavior of a stock or an index. For example, intraday volatility will be larger than its close-close counterpart when large price changes occur during the daily trading session. Additionally, since the close-close calculation includes all price changes, it must also be the case that the large spikes causing the distortion tend to reverse before the close. The behavior is characteristic of stocks that are excellent day trading candidates. Furthermore, because large intraday swings are almost never priced into option contracts, they are often excellent long straddle candidates as well. The opposite is true when intraday volatility levels are reduced because the largest price spikes must be occurring in the after- or pre-market sessions, where they are invisible to the intraday calculation. In such cases, the stock tends to experience large changes at the open and reduced activity during the trading session. Options on these stocks tend to be fairly priced because the largest changes are comprehended by traditional close-close volatility calculations.

Price-change data expressed in dollars and cents has limited value when the goal is to compare different securities. The traditional solution has been to compare percent changes so that a $5 price change for a $100 stock is equivalent to a $1 change for a $20 stock. This method also has drawbacks because a $5 price change for a very volatile $100 stock would be much more likely than a $1 price change for a $20 stock with very low historical volatility. We can use information about historical volatility to level this playing field by measuring each price change in standard deviations against the most recent volatility window. In this regard, it is important that each price change be measured against a window that ends just ahead of the change so that the change being measured does not influence the calculation. If the change being measured were part of the calculation, the value would be distorted, and the size of the distortion would be inversely proportional to the length of the window. Table 2.8 illustrates the price-spike-calculation process. Once again, our example is based on a window containing 20 price changes. Consequently, the first calculation will measure the price change for record 22 against the standard deviation of the changes for records 2–21. The steps required to calculate the first value (-0.96) are outlined here:

1. Calculate the standard deviation of the 20 price changes immediately preceding the spike (days 2–21). The value obtained is the 1-day volatility at the end of the first 20 price-change window. **result = 0.0188**

2. Multiply this number by the value of the close on day 21 ($86.31) to determine the magnitude of a 1 standard deviation price change at the end of the window. **result = $1.62**

3. Divide the day 22 price change (-$1.55) by this value to recast the change in standard deviations. **result = -0.96**

After each calculation, the window is advanced 1 day and the next price change is measured against the new window. Table 2.8 displays results for 3 complete calculations in the column labeled Spike.

TABLE 2.8   *Illustrated price spike calculation.*

	A	B	C	D	E	F	G
1	Close	Price Chng($)	Log Chng	Daily Volat	1 StdDev($)	Spike	Description
2	86.47						
3	88.60	2.13	0.0243				
4	90.31	1.71	0.0191				
5	91.63	1.32	0.0145				
6	89.54	-2.09	-0.0231				
7	91.81	2.27	0.0250				
8	91.80	-0.01	-0.0001				
9	91.66	-0.14	-0.0015				
10	91.32	-0.34	-0.0037				
11	91.12	-0.20	-0.0022				
12	91.27	0.15	0.0016				
13	89.83	-1.44	-0.0159				
14	87.04	-2.79	-0.0316				
15	88.26	1.22	0.0139				
16	88.75	0.49	0.0055				
17	86.14	-2.61	-0.0298				
18	89.05	2.91	0.0332				
19	88.55	-0.50	-0.0056				
20	87.72	-0.83	-0.0094				
21	85.47	-2.25	-0.0260				
22	86.31	0.84	0.0098	0.0188	1.62	-0.96	
23	84.76	-1.55	-0.0181	0.0183	1.55	-1.20	B23/E22
24	82.90	-1.86	-0.0222	0.0181	1.50	-0.47	B24/E23
	22.00	0.70	0.0095	0.0175	1.44		B25/E24

Column G is included for clarity only. It delineates the 3 calculations visible in cells F23–F25. We could also have compressed columns D, E, and F into a single calculation. For example, the value contained in cell F23 is given by

`B23/(STDEV(C3:C22)*A22)`

As always, the statement can be expanded to include a conditional that checks to make sure that a single window does not cross tickers. Table 2.9 displays the final form. It has been abbreviated for purposes of space by using a shorter window (5 days) for the price spike calculation. The table includes data for 2 different tickers. As before, an additional column is included that contains descriptive information (column F). Readers will notice that row 10 is blank in columns C and D where the ticker transition occurs. These blanks are the result of a conditional that was added to the front of each price-change calculation that leaves the respective cell blank if the tickers are mismatched:

Column C—`IF(B9=B10,B10-B9,"")`

Column D—`IF(B9=B10,LN(B10/B9),"")`

However, the results displayed in column E will not be altered if a price change is recorded for a ticker transition—the mistake will simply be ignored.

TABLE 2.9   *Illustrated price spike calculation—multiple tickers.*

	A	B	C	D	E	F
1	Symbol	Close	Price Chng($)	Log Chng	Spike	Description—Column E
2	AAA	86.47				
3	AAA	88.60	2.13	0.0243		
4	AAA	90.31	1.71	0.0191		
5	AAA	91.63	1.32	0.0145		
6	AAA	89.54	-2.09	-0.0231		
7	AAA	91.81	2.27	0.0250		
8	AAA	91.80	-0.01	-0.0001	-0.0054	IF(A2=A8,C8/(STDEV(D3:D7)*B7),"")
9	AAA	91.66	-0.14	-0.0015	-0.0792	IF(A3=A9,C9/(STDEV(D4:D8)*B8),"")
10	BBB	120.19				
11	BBB	120.38	0.19	0.0016		
12	BBB	117.5	-2.88	-0.0242		
13	BBB	118.75	1.25	0.0106		
14	BBB	120.5	1.75	0.0146		
15	BBB	125.09	4.59	0.0374		
16	BBB	123.66	-1.43	-0.0115	-0.5121	IF(A10=A16,C16/(STDEV(D11:D15)*B15),"")
17	BBB	121.55	-2.11	-0.0172	-0.7119	IF(A11=A17,C17/(STDEV(D12:D16)*B16),"")

Each series of price changes can be visualized using standard bar charts. Because the data has been recast in standard deviations, direct comparisons between charts for different securities can provide meaningful insights. Furthermore, each chart can include a large number of data points and it is often possible to quickly gain significant insights just by viewing the data. Figure 2.1 displays 2 years (500 days) of price-change data for gold.

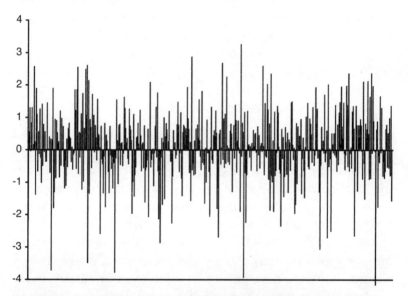

FIGURE 2.1   *Price-change history for gold 12/20/2005–12/14/2007 (500 days). Y-axis in standard deviations measured against the most recent 20-day volatility window.*

During the time frame of the chart, gold prices climbed from $490 to more than $800. However, despite the bullish nature of the commodity, downward price spikes tended to be considerably larger than upward ones. This dynamic translates into large downward corrections that are difficult to hedge against. Furthermore, put-call parity prevents option pricing discrepancies that would compensate for such imbalances. From a risk-adjusted perspective, calls were overpriced and puts were underpriced throughout the time frame of the chart. We can also remove much of the noise and simplify the image by filtering changes smaller than 1 standard deviation. The adjustment is easily accomplished with a conditional statement that copies the price changes into a new column and replaces values smaller than 1 standard deviation with a null character. Using this technique, we can choose to view any size or range of sizes and quickly determine the frequency.

Descriptive Ratios

It is relatively easy to create the common building blocks of most technical charting strategies and to store them as additional columns in the worksheet. While re-creating these charting methods is outside our primary focus, the basic elements include descriptive ratios that can be used in a variety of ways. One solution that has proven to be very flexible is to create the elements used for candlestick charting. Candlestick patterns are often used to study equities and futures because each chart element contains a surprising amount of information. Every modern charting package includes a candlestick option, and Excel can automatically generate candlestick charts from 4 consecutive columns that include open, high, low, and closing prices. Figure 2.2 displays the basic structure of a single candle in 2 versions—up and down. By convention, up candles are hollow and down candles are shaded. The top of the body marks the close for an up candle and the open for a down candle. The lower shadow, sometimes referred to as the "tail," marks the low; the upper shadow, sometimes called the "hair," marks the high.

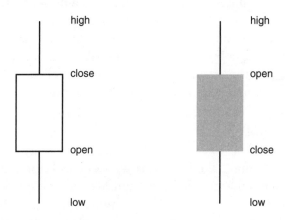

FIGURE 2.2   *Basic candle structure*

Our goal is to break down each day's candle into individual components, and to store the value of each component in a separate column of the worksheet. The result is a set of descriptive ratios that can be used to sort, analyze, and further describe historical prices. Furthermore, the same analytical techniques can be used to study any time frame—daily, weekly, monthly, quarterly, hourly, or minute-by-minute.

Suppose, for example, we decided to test the theory that candles characterized by a small body and long shadows tend to be followed by large price swings. Candles that display this characteristic are commonly referred to as "spinning tops." The simple solution is to calculate the percentage of the total candle represented by the body: ABS(open-close)/(high-low). We use the absolute value function (ABS) to accommodate up candles where the close is higher than the open. Assuming one of our columns contains this information, we can design many different experiments to study the effects of increasingly small open-to-close differences as measured against high-low. One interesting variation involves searching for consecutive spinning top candles and observing the price-change behavior that follows. The search would be accomplished using conditionals that specify a threshold for filtering records followed by a test to confirm consecutive matching ticker symbols.

The most straightforward solution is to use Excel's AND function, which returns the logical value TRUE when its arguments are all true and FALSE when one or more arguments are false. By nesting 2 AND functions we can check for values that meet our spinning top criterion and also compare ticker symbols. If column G contains the spinning top ratio mentioned previously, the following comparison would test for a value less than 0.25 in rows 2 and 3:

```
AND(G3 < 0.25, G2 < 0.25)
```

With ticker symbols in column A, the second nested AND function can be added to confirm matching symbols for the 2 rows:

```
AND(AND(G3 < 0.25, G2 < 0.25),A3 = A2)
```

Finally, the statement can be extended with an IF conditional that yields a value of 1 when true and a blank (null) value when false:

```
IF(AND(AND(G3 < 0.25, G2 < 0.25),A3 = A2),1,"")
```

This approach is often preferable to creating a column containing the words "TRUE" or "FALSE" for each record.

It is now possible to sort the results and group together all records whose calculations yield a value of 1. However, the sort will destroy the order upon which the calculations are based. As always, the process can be reversed simply by clicking the "undo typing" arrow or by executing a new sort based on ticker and date. A logical approach is to group records that meet the test criteria, manually mark interesting records for further study, and then reverse the process so that records are again ordered by ticker and date. The effect can then be studied by retrieving follow on records for each event. A representative table with flagged records is displayed in Table 2.10. The test criteria were designed to select the second record in each pair where the candle body was less than 20% of the high-low for both records.

TABLE 2.10   *Consecutive pairs of spinning top candles.*

	A	B	C	D	E	F	G	H
1	Symbol	Day	O	H	L	C	Body %	Test
2	AAA	20061120	85.40	87.00	85.20	86.47	0.594	
3	AAA	20061121	87.42	88.60	87.11	88.60	0.792	
4	AAA	20061122	88.99	90.75	87.85	89.12	0.045	
5	AAA	20061124	89.53	93.08	89.50	91.63	0.587	
6	AAA	20061127	92.51	93.16	89.50	92.45	0.016	
7	AAA	20061128	90.36	91.97	89.91	90.75	0.189	1
8	AAA	20061129	93.00	93.15	90.25	91.80	0.414	
9	BBB	20061120	92.22	92.68	91.06	91.66	0.346	
10	BBB	20061121	91.80	92.33	90.10	91.50	0.135	
11	BBB	20061122	91.88	92.05	90.50	91.12	0.490	
12	BBB	20061124	91.66	92.33	90.87	91.27	0.267	
13	BBB	20061127	90.65	91.39	89.67	90.35	0.174	
14	BBB	20061128	90.03	90.50	86.90	90.00	0.008	1
15	BBB	20061129	87.23	89.39	87.00	88.26	0.431	

Figure 2.3 displays the candles for each entry in the table. Arrows mark the records flagged in rows 7 and 14.

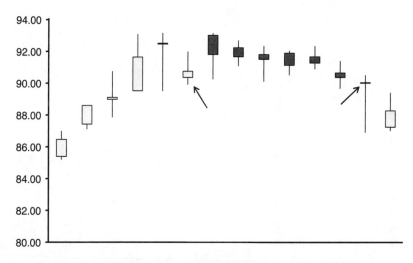

FIGURE 2.3　*Candlestick chart for Table 2.10. Arrows mark flagged records from the table.*

Our example is one of many possible scenarios that can be executed against a fully enumerated set of candle parameters. Table 2.11 lists the complete set of calculations for both up (close > open) and down (open > close) records.

TABLE 2.11　*Calculations that generate fully enumerated candle parameters.*

	Up Candle (Close > Open)	Down Candle (Open > Close)
Upper Shadow	high - close	high - open
Upper Shadow %	(high - close) / (high - low)	(high - open) / (high - low)
Lower Shadow	open - low	close - low
Lower Shadow %	(open - low) / (high - low)	(close - low) / (high - low)
Body	close - open	open - close
Body %	(close - open) / (high - low)	(open - close) / (high - low)

The information contained in Table 2.11 would add 6 columns to our price history worksheet, which now contains the following information arranged in columns:

Basic Information	Calculated Values
Symbol	Decimal date
Date	Weekday
Open	90-day volatility
High	20-day volatility
Low	Price-spike size (StdDev)
Close	6 candle parameters
Volume	

These data items are meant as examples and there are obviously many more possibilities. Some are available from data providers. One notable example is short interest, which is known to strongly influence the way that stocks react to financial news. We might also build parallel tables containing economic data, currency exchange rates, bond yields, commodity prices, and information gleaned from news releases. Unfortunately, a collection of related worksheets is difficult to design and maintain. The solution is to create a database containing logically linked tables and associated programs for statistically analyzing and summarizing the data. This type of infrastructure will be the focus of our next chapter.

We can also create summary tables directly from our price history worksheet without leaving Excel. This approach makes sense when the goal is to summarize a large number of records contained in a single worksheet. The next section will provide examples of summary programs written in Visual Basic. While specific programming details are important, readers are encouraged to focus on the general flow and logic.

Creating Summary Tables

Summarizing a large worksheet invariably involves writing a Visual Basic program. The complexity can vary from a simple macro containing just a few lines of code to a sophisticated commercial-grade application. The simple approach is usually best, and it is relatively easy to construct a library of small special-purpose applications that each accomplish a precisely defined task. Additionally, because the goal is to tabulate results and create a summary, the major focus should be the underlying logic associated with storing cell locations, counting records, tracking ticker symbols, and a small number of simple calculations. It is not necessary to invoke advanced mathematical functions, design end-user interfaces, or write long, complex statements. With regard to the last item, the complexity of individual statements can be greatly diminished when we introduce the flexibility of a program. Our previous price-spike calculation serves as a contrasting example. Each statement determined the standard deviation across a predetermined window, multiplied this value by the closing price to determine the value of a 1 standard deviation price change, retrieved the next record's price change, divided this change by the value of 1 standard deviation, verified matching tickers at the beginning and end of the window, and made a decision to write a value or a null character. Considering the level of functionality, the statements were surprisingly simple. However, in a Visual basic program we have the option of splitting long, complex statements into simpler steps and storing calculated values so they can be reused. Excel VBA applications can also execute any function that can be written for a single cell using the WorksheetFunction object. These characteristics allow us to rapidly create simple but powerful programs and to focus our attention on the underlying logic. Most important, we are not limited by the amount of functionality that can be included in a single statement.

Table 2.12 displays a sample summary table for data organized in the style depicted in Table 2.9. Each row in the table contains a breakdown of the number of price spikes in various size classes for a single ticker (0.5 StdDev–4.0 StdDev in increments of 0.5 StdDev). By creating a summary of this form, we gain the ability to review data for hundreds of tickers that each span significant lengths of time.

TABLE 2.12   Summary table format—price spikes organized by ticker. See Listing 2.5.

Ticker	>0.5 StdDev	>1.0 StdDev	>1.5 StdDev	>2.0 StdDev	>2.5 StdDev	>3.0 StdDev	>3.5 StdDev	>4.0 StdDev
AAAA	42	26	16	10	5	5	3	2
BBBB	54	31	18	10	2	1	1	0
CCCC	62	35	19	10	3	2	1	1
DDDD	61	32	18	7	2	2	2	2

Listing 2.5 displays the Excel VBA program that created Table 2.12 from a sample dataset composed of 4 tickers each containing 100 records. Input data for the program was organized in columns as follows: (A) Symbol, (B) Date, (C) Close, (D) Price Change, (E) Log Price Change, and (F) Spike in StdDev. Although not essential, column B (Date) has been added to the format because a thorough analysis generally involves aligning records by date and removing incomplete tickers. Consistency across a dataset is especially important when the goal is to measure the frequency of price spikes in various size classes. Two versions of the program are included. The first, displayed in Listing 2.5, summarizes price-spike data already stored in column F. Listing 2.6 extends these capabilities with additional steps that calculate the price-spike size for each record. This version of the program needs only closing prices as input because it calculates price changes, log price changes, and price spikes in standard deviations before creating a summary.

LISTING 2.5 *Excel VBA price-spike-summary program.*

```
 1: Sub spikes()
 2: Dim DataRow As Long
 3: Dim SummaryRow As Long
 4: Dim LastDataRow As Long
 5: Dim ReferenceTicker As String
 6: Dim Count As Integer
 7: Dim Criterion As Double
 8: Dim IterationIndex As Integer
 9: Dim ScoreColumnName As String
10: Dim SummaryColumn_2 As Integer
11: Dim RangeString As String

12: IterationIndex = 0
13: For Criterion = 0.5 To 4 Step 0.5
```

```
14: DataRow = 2
15: Count = 0
16: ReferenceTicker = Cells(DataRow, "A")

'Create a sum for each ticker and store in column G
17: While Cells(DataRow, "A") <> ""
18:  If Cells(DataRow, "A") = ReferenceTicker Then
19:    If Abs(Cells(DataRow, "F")) > Criterion Then
20:      Count = Count + 1
21:    End If
22:  Else
23:    ReferenceTicker = Cells(DataRow, "A")
24:    DataRow = DataRow - 1
25:    Cells(DataRow, "G") = Count
26:    Count = 0
27:  End If
28: DataRow = DataRow + 1
29: Wend
30: Cells(DataRow - 1, "G") = Count

'Create summary table-add data after each pass through the file
31: LastDataRow = DataRow - 1
32: SummaryRow = DataRow + 2
33: ScoreColumnName = ">" & Criterion & " StdDev"
34: SummaryColumn_2 = IterationIndex + 2
35: Cells(SummaryRow, SummaryColumn_2) = ScoreColumnName
36: If IterationIndex = 0 Then
37:  Cells(SummaryRow, "A") = "Ticker"
38: End If
39: SummaryRow = SummaryRow + 1

40: For DataRow = 2 To LastDataRow
41:  If Cells(DataRow, "G") <> "" Then
42:    Cells(SummaryRow, "A") = Cells(DataRow, "A")
43:    Cells(SummaryRow, SummaryColumn_2) = Cells(DataRow, "G")
44:    SummaryRow = SummaryRow + 1
45:  End If
46: Next DataRow
```

```
'Begin next pass through the file
47: IterationIndex = IterationIndex + 1
48: Next Criterion

'Format summary table
49: RangeString = "A" & (LastDataRow + 4) & _
    ":" & "I" & (SummaryRow - 1)
50: Range(RangeString).Select
51: Selection.NumberFormat = "0"

52: End Sub
```

The program is divided into 2 major sections. The first, contained in lines 17–30, scans the file, counting the number of spikes above the current threshold (set in line 13) and storing the results in column G at the end of each ticker. Line 30 backs up 1 row to store the final result after the last record in the file has been encountered. The second section, contained in lines 31–46, adds data to the summary table after each pass through the file. An independent variable (IterationIndex) serves as a pointer to the column that will be modified after each pass through the data. The major program loop, which begins in line 13 and ends in line 48, terminates after the 4 standard deviation spikes have been tabulated. Line 13 can be altered to vary the criteria, and the program will automatically accommodate the changes.

Each pass through the data begins by recording the contents of cell A2 as a reference ticker in line 16. The While loop that immediately follows checks successive records against the reference. If the tickers match, and the absolute value of the price spike recorded in column F exceeds the criterion, then the count is incremented. Conversely, if the test in line 18 reveals that the new ticker does not match the reference, then the following sequence of events is executed in lines 23–26:

Line 23—A new reference ticker is stored in
ReferenceTicker.

Line 24—The row pointer is moved back 1 row to the end of the previous ticker.

Line 25—The current count is stored in column G.

Line 26—The count is reset to zero before advancing to the first row of the next ticker.

Moving the row pointer back in line 24 is preferable to modifying line 25 because the row pointer will once again be advanced (line 28) before the next loop is executed. Modifying line 25 to store data in the previous row leaves the pointer at the beginning of the next ticker, and line 28 moves the pointer forward so that the first line is not read. In most situations the first record is part of a calculation window and does not contain a price spike. However, the first record becomes significant if blank records have been removed prior to generating the summary. These details highlight the importance of exhaustive testing under a variety of circumstances. Unlike most computer programs, algorithms that generate summary tables from complex datasets have the potential to operate properly under one set of conditions and fail under another. It is not uncommon to use a program for some time before discovering a subtle problem that yields a calculation error.

Once the final count is stored at the end of the last ticker in the file (line 30), the row pointer is advanced and the summary table is created. Line 31 records the final row of the last ticker, and line 32 sets a pointer for the beginning of the first row of the summary table. Line 33 assembles a string that contains the column heading for the current pass. For example, the third pass counts spikes greater than 1.5 standard deviations so the appropriate string is > 1.5 StdDev. If IterationIndex = 0 (first pass through the dataset), then the upper-left corner of the summary table is given the heading Ticker in line 37. The core logic for this section is contained in lines 40–46. The file is sequentially searched for results which are stored at the end of each ticker in column G. Each result is captured and copied into the summary table (lines 42–43). The SummaryRow pointer is incremented after each record (line 44) and the program continues scanning for the next available value in column G. This process continues until the final row is encountered. IterationIndex is advanced and the next major program loop is launched (lines 47–48).

Once the summary table is complete, the cells can be formatted to eliminate decimal places since all the numbers are integers. Steps 49–51 accomplish this task using Excel's Select method and Range object. Lines 49 and 50 can be combined into a single step but they are separated here for clarity. Once the range that spans the space between the upper-left and lower-right corners of the table has been selected, the new number format can be set to 0 decimal places (line 51). The program terminates after this formatting operation. Although not necessary for the calculations, these steps are included because they illustrate the use of the important and often used Range object.

We will complete this discussion by automating the steps that calculate values for columns D–F (price change, log price change, and price spikes in standard deviations). The program described earlier is designed to operate on a worksheet that already contains this information—presumably generated using Excel functions as previously described. However, we can eliminate the manual steps by enhancing our program with a few lines of code that execute these calculations. The details are displayed in Listing 2.6.

LISTING 2.6   *Extensions to Listing 2.5 for calculating price spikes.*

```
1: Dim WindowLength As Integer
2: Dim StdDevRange As Range

3: WindowLength = 20

  'Column headings
4: Cells(1, "A") = "Symbol"
5: Cells(1, "B") = "Date"
6: Cells(1, "C") = "Close"
7: Cells(1, "D") = "Price Change"
8: Cells(1, "E") = "Log Change"
9: Cells(1, "F") = "Spike"

  'Calculate price change and log of price change
10: DataRow = 3
11: While Cells(DataRow, "A") <> ""
12:  If Cells(DataRow, "A") = Cells(DataRow - 1, "A") Then
13:    Cells(DataRow, "D") = Cells(DataRow, "C") - _
       Cells(DataRow - 1, "C")
14:    Cells(DataRow, "E") = Log(Cells(DataRow, "C") / _
       Cells(DataRow - 1, "C"))
15:  End If
16: DataRow = DataRow + 1
17: Wend

  'Calculate price spikes in standard deviations
18: DataRow = WindowLength + 3
19: While Cells(DataRow, "A") <> ""
20:  If Cells(DataRow, "A") = Cells(DataRow - _
     WindowLength - 1, "A") Then
21:    Set StdDevRange = Range("E" & (DataRow - _
       WindowLength) & ":" & "E" & (DataRow - 1))
22:    Cells(DataRow, "F") = Cells(DataRow, "D") / _
       (Application.WorksheetFunction.StDev(StdDevRange) _
       * Cells(DataRow - 1, "C"))
23:  End If
```

```
24:   DataRow = DataRow + 1
25:   Wend
```

The 25 lines of code contained in this listing can be pasted in front of the program detailed in Listing 2.5. Only 2 new variables need to be added—WindowLength, which sets the length of the volatility window, and StdDevRange, which is assigned to a range of cells defined by this length. This range object is then used by the standard deviation worksheet function to identify the beginning and end of the window over which the calculation takes place (line 22). StdDevRange is upgraded in line 21 with new beginning and ending cells before each pass through the file.

Altering the value of WindowLength in line 3 changes the length of the window used for volatility calculations. The remainder of the program will adapt to the change and no other adjustments are necessary. Lines 10–17 contain the logic for calculating each price change and the log of each price change. Row 3 of the worksheet is set as the starting point because it contains the second record (first price change). Line 11 checks for the end of the file and line 12 compares tickers to ensure that the calculation is valid. The price change to be stored in column D is generated in line 13. Likewise, the log of the price change that is stored in column E is generated in line 14.

A similar process (lines 18–25) is used to generate the price-spike calculations that are stored in column F. The pointer is initially advanced to the row where the calculation will be stored, which is 1 row beyond the end of the volatility window (line 18). The statement in line 20 checks to make sure that the first record in the series (initially row 2 of the worksheet) contains the same ticker as the row where the calculation will be stored. Readers will note that for 20 price changes the test spans 22 records. Table 2.13 contains a list of the rows involved in the first price-spike calculation near the top of the worksheet. The third column contains a corresponding list of pointers for program steps 18–25. Each pointer is based on the DataRow variable, which is set to WindowLength+3 in line 18 of the program. The table is meant to clarify the use of the DataRow variable in lines 18–25.

TABLE 2.13   *Logistics of the* DataRow *variable in lines 18–25 of Listing 2.6.*

Row	Contents	Pointer for Lines 18–25
1	Column headings	DataRow - WindowLength - 2
2	First closing price	DataRow - WindowLength - 1
3	First price change in volatility window	DataRow - WindowLength
22	Last price change in volatility window	DataRow - 1
23	Price change to be compared to volatility window	DataRow

Line 21 of the program creates a string that defines the range object for the current window, and line 22 calculates the price spike for the record that follows. The statement in line 22 is complex. It calculates the standard deviation for the range, multiplies this value by the closing price in column C to determine the value of a 1 standard deviation price change, and divides the next record's price change (column D) by this value. Results are stored in column F. Readers are encouraged to verify that the logic matches that used to create the values stored in column E of Table 2.9 (detailed descriptions of the calculations appear in column F of the table).

The underlying logic of this program is particularly relevant because it tends to reappear in many places where the goal is to count and tabulate results. The combined version which consists of only 77 lines of programming can calculate a moving volatility window of any length across a dataset consisting of multiple tickers and use this information to build a table of price spikes that spans all records for all tickers. Blank records in the first window of each ticker can be removed by sorting the spreadsheet on column F, deleting records that lack a value, and resorting by ticker and date. This operation is useful when the goal is to create a table of price spikes that does not contain any intervening spaces.

Listing 2.5 embodies logic that can form the basis of many different strategies for creating summary tables. Moreover, the core logic of the program occupies only about 30 lines of programming. These characteristics are helpful when the goal is to develop a library of routines for summarizing different datasets. The logic can also be embedded in a set of callable functions that can be referenced by larger, more complex programs. Generally speaking, when the goal is to analyze historical data for investment purposes, the simplest approach should win out over the most elegant. These programs were written with this theme in mind; simplicity and clarity were chosen over efficiency.

Discovering Statistical Correlations

Equities that display similar behavior can be identified using data visualization techniques. One of the most straightforward and commonly used analysis techniques involves construction of a simple scatterplot where each point represents the prices of 2 different stocks on a particular day; one assigned to the x-axis and one to the y-axis. For each point, position relative to the main diagonal (the identity line) directly relates the relative difference between 2 price changes. Stocks that exhibit identical behavior appear on the identity line, while differently behaved stocks exhibit price points that are scattered around the line. For example, the points x=50:y=100, x=51:y=102, and x=52:y=104 fall directly on the identity line, while x=50:y=100 and x=51:y=102, and x=52:y=105 do not. In the second case, the $105 price point represented a proportionally larger price change than its $52 counterpart. Points that appear above the diagonal represent large price changes for the stock mapped to the y-axis; conversely, points that appear below the diagonal represent relatively large price changes for the stock on the x-axis. Figure 2.4 contains a scatterplot for 2 stocks, Apple Computer (AAPL) and Research in Motion (RIMM), that displayed remarkably similar price-change profiles during the time frame of the chart (9/4/2007–11/30/2007).

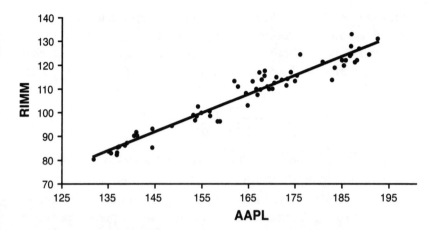

FIGURE 2.4 *Scatterplot for 2 closely related stocks. AAPL is represented on the x-axis and RIMM on the y-axis. Time frame of the chart is 9/4/2007–11/30/2007.*

We can quantitatively express the extent to which the 2 datasets are related by calculating a correlation coefficient. There are many different types of correlation measurements, each suited to comparing different types of data. To determine which is best for a specific experiment, it is necessary to know the type of scale used to express each data series, the nature of the underlying distribution (continuous or discrete), and whether the distribution is linear or nonlinear. Because it is designed to measure the strength of the linear relationship between 2 variables, the Pearson product-moment correlation coefficient, often referred to as "Pearson r," is well suited to the task of comparing the price series displayed in Figure 2.4.

Stated in words, the Pearson correlation represents the extent to which an event occupies the same relative position on two variables. It is obtained by dividing the covariance of the two variables by the product of their standard deviations. The formula is

$$\frac{\Sigma(X\text{-}Xa)(Y\text{-}Ya)}{\sqrt{\Sigma(X\text{-}Xa)^2\ \Sigma(Y\text{-}Ya)^2}}$$

where (X - Xa) and (Y - Ya) represent the deviations of each price from the mean of the corresponding series.

The calculation yields a dimensionless number that ranges from +1 to -1. A correlation of +1 indicates a perfect positive linear relationship between the two datasets; a correlation of -1 indicates a perfect negative linear. Although rare, a correlation of exactly 0 means there is no linear relationship. The Pearson correlation coefficient for the two series displayed in Figure 2.4 is 0.97. As is apparent in the figure, it is not necessary that the scales be identical. A correlation of -0.97 would have been visualized as a negative sloping line where rising values on the x-axis correlate with falling values on the y-axis.

Excel's PEARSON function can be used to compare a large number of individual tickers organized into vertical columns. The most straightforward strategy involves creating a matrix that compares each symbol to every other member of the group. Table 2.14A contains data for an abbreviated example and Table 2.14B contains the correlation matrix and actual results. The example is structured around 6 ticker symbols (T1–T6).

TABLE 2.14A   *Data for Pearson r calculation for 6 tickers (T1–T6) spanning 10 days. See Table 2.14B for correlation logistics and actual results.*

	A	B	C	D	E	F
	T1	**T2**	**T3**	**T4**	**T5**	**T6**
1	T1	T2	T3	T4	T5	T6
2	144.16	134.78	118.97	136.21	87.10	107.96
3	136.76	136.18	114.57	134.15	85.13	107.50
4	135.01	136.93	114.69	135.20	86.49	107.39
5	131.77	135.50	111.49	132.15	83.31	108.52
6	136.71	137.83	110.48	132.25	83.87	108.31
7	135.49	138.28	110.85	134.92	85.64	106.95
8	136.85	139.21	108.36	135.40	85.10	106.69
9	137.20	138.76	109.12	136.90	85.79	107.58
10	138.81	139.47	109.90	137.17	85.93	106.16
11	138.41	138.61	108.62	136.30	86.46	104.90

TABLE 2.14B   *Correlation matrix and actual results for Table 2.14A. The strongest correlations, (T4:T5) and (T2:T3), are highlighted in boldface type.*

Comparisons

T1:T2	**T2:T3**	T3:T4	**T4:T5**	T5:T6
T1:T3	T2:T4	T3:T5	T4:T6	
T1:T4	T2:T5	T3:T6		
T1:T5	T2:T6			
T1:T6				

Pearson Correlation Coefficients

-0.0815	**-0.8462**	-0.0591	**0.8410**	-0.5045
0.4209	0.4340	0.3548	-0.6299	
0.6024	0.0654	0.4627		
0.7018	-0.6345			
-0.2216				

Excel's syntax for calculating the Pearson correlation between T1 and T2 is this:

```
PEARSON(A2:A11,B2:B11)
```

Table 2.14B extends the comparison matrix to include all combinations of tickers from T1:T2 to T1:T6. Using absolute row references simplifies cutting and pasting operations:

PEARSON(A$2:A$11,B$2:B$11)

Once the table is complete, Excel's MAX and MIN functions can be used to identify key results across the entire range. For example, if the Pearson correlation matrix in Table 2.14B spans columns O–S and rows 2–6, the maximum value in the table can be found using the following:

MAX(O2:S6)

In this case O2 is the upper-left corner of the matrix, and S6, which does not contain a value, is the lower-right. The maximum value in the table is 0.8410—a strong correlation that corresponds to tickers T4:T5. An equally strong negative correlation was found between tickers T2:T3 (-0.8462). Virtually no correlation was found between ticker pairs T1:T2, T3:T4, T2:T5.

This information can help guide portfolio construction when the goal is to balance risk and hedge one investment against another. In practice each comparison would include many more rows and the table would likely compare many more tickers. It would be perfectly reasonable to construct a comparison between 50 different tickers that each contain a year of closing prices. Different experiments can also be designed using different date ranges.

Large complex comparisons can be simplified by clustering together symbols that display similar behavior. This approach is routinely used by molecular biologists studying gene expression profiles that include many individual sequences. Such experiments often require thousands of comparisons, and the results are most meaningful when sequences are organized into a hierarchical cluster. For example, Table 2.14B could be simplified by creating new composite tickers composed of T2:T3 and T4:T5—the two most closely related pairs. Another round of comparisons would then be executed using T1, T2:T3, T4:T5, and T6. We can repeat the process by constructing new hybrid tickers from the most closely correlated pairs and executing additional comparisons. As the clustering process progresses, a tree structure can be constructed to display links between individual tickers and combinations of tickers. Each correlation coefficient can be thought of as representing the Euclidean distance between two items in the matrix. The correlations are ordered and nodes created between the highest-scoring (geometrically closest) pairs. The matrix is then modified to represent the joined elements as a single node, and all distances between the newly formed node and other items in the matrix are calculated. It is not necessary to recalculate all correlations since only those involving the two items joined in the new node are changed. A diagram can be created where each node is represented by a link, the height of the link being directly proportional to the strength of the correlation. Such diagrams are sometimes referred to as dendrograms. The process of creating proportional links and joining tickers into clusters can be continued until all tickers have been joined into a single hierarchy through links of appropriate length. Caution is advised because characteristics of individual symbols become less relevant as the clustering process progresses; it is not generally reasonable to extend the hierarchy more than 1 or 2 levels beyond the initial correlation matrix.

This method of building a hierarchy by measuring the geometric distance between tickers and recursively clustering together those that are most closely related can be a useful tool for portfolio management and, in particular, for hedging. Tickers that behave in a coherent fashion can be grouped together and hedged as a single entity using short calls, long puts, or short stock on any member of the group. A relatively simple example is displayed in Tables 2.15A and 2.15B, which contain initial correlations and a primary hierarchy that clusters together three similarly behaved tickers. Each table contains a legend designed to overlap with the correlation matrix. Tickers T1–T10 and composite C1 refer to the following tickers spanning the time frame 9/4/2007–11/30/2007:

T1	AAPL	T6	RIG	C1	AAPL-RIMM-GOOG
T2	ACL	T7	RIMM		
T3	AZO	T8	SPY		
T4	FXY	T9	TM		
T5	SHLD	T10	GOOG		

TABLE 2.15A Pearson correlation matrix for 10 tickers. Strongest positive and negative correlations are represented in boldface type. Results are used to build a first-round hierarchy, displayed in Table 2.15B.

Pair	Value	Pair	Value	Pair	Value	Pair	Value	Pair	Value	Pair	Value	Pair	Value	Pair	Value	Pair	Value
T1:T2	0.589	**T2:T3**	**0.837**	T3:T4	-0.696	**T4:T5**	**-0.896**	T5:T6	-0.674	T6:T7	0.669	T7:T8	0.135	T8:T9	0.398	T9:T10	-0.49
T1:T3	0.402	T2:T4	-0.446	T3:T5	0.752	T4:T6	0.641	T5:T7	-0.121	T6:T8	-0.353	T7:T9	-0.429	T9:T10	-0.068		
T1:T4	0.226	T2:T5	0.473	T3:T6	-0.194	T4:T7	0.187	T5:T8	0.783	T6:T9	-0.280	**T7:T10**	**0.956**				
T1:T5	-0.182	T2:T6	-0.013	T3:T7	0.427	**T4:T8**	**-0.885**	T5:T9	0.342	T6:T10	0.786						
T1:T6	0.683	T2:T7	0.615	**T3:T8**	**0.821**	T4:T9	-0.461	T5:T10	-0.324								
T1:T7	**0.969**	T2:T8	0.653	T3:T9	0.097	T4:T10	0.386										
T1:T8	0.105	T2:T9	-0.158	T3:T10	0.265												
T1:T9	-0.439	T2:T10	0.496														
T1:T10	**0.964**																

Strong positive correlations are revealed between three tickers—AAPL, RIMM, and GOOG. Conversely, strong negative correlations are apparent between FXY (Japanese Yen Trust) and the broad market as represented by the S&P 500 (SPY) in addition to FXY and Sears (SHLD). Additionally, FXY displays only one significant positive correlation with another ticker (FXY:RIG = 0.641). Based on these results, we can create a new matrix that combines the 3 closely related tickers (AAPL, RIMM, and GOOG) and excludes FXY. Table 2.15B displays the results of the first hierarchy.

TABLE 2.15B   *Pearson correlation matrix for a first-pass hierarchy based on Table 2.15A. The strongest correlations are highlighted in boldface type.*

0.837	0.752	-0.674	-0.353	0.398	-0.458
0.473	-0.194	0.783	-0.280	0.056	
-0.013	**0.821**	0.342	0.723		
0.653	0.097	-0.215			
-0.158	0.368				
0.573					
T2:T3	T3:T5	T5:T6	T6:T8	T8:T9	T9:C1
T2:T5	T3:T6	T5:T8	T6:T9	T8:C1	
T2:T6	**T3:T8**	T5:T9	T6:C1		
T2:T8	T3:T9	T5:C1			
T2:T9	T3:C1				
T2:C1					

Only a single ticker, RIG, displays a significant correlation with the new composite C1. The hierarchy construction process can be continued by extending C1 to include RIG, and by clustering together the symbol pairs represented in the slightly weaker correlations ACL:AZO and AZO:SPY that are highlighted in both tables.

Hierarchical clustering is designed to comprehend many data points spanning extended periods of time. Tables 2.15A and 2.15B, for example, compared 62 price changes for 10 stocks. Such comparisons are helpful when the goal is to identify broad correlations that tend to be persistent. However, more precise comparisons that characterize the responses of individual stocks to a very limited number of specific events can be powerful predictive tools. In this context, our previous example can be thought of as a 10-stock comparison under 62 different sets of market conditions. Since most of the 62 days were unremarkable, the results tend to blur many important distinctions. Stocks that display relatively strong parallel behavior across extended time frames can have markedly different responses to specific market conditions.

A meaningful experiment can be constructed by comparing the responses of a group of stocks to 2 different sets of market conditions. For the purpose of this discussion, we will select 2 days when the markets experienced dramatic moves in opposite directions. The goal will be to group stocks according to their responses to both events.

The first day (7/24/2007) was characterized by the steepest decline in 4 years of U.S. stocks as fears that a subprime lending crisis was beginning to spill over into the broad economy. Countrywide Financial Corp., the largest U.S. mortgage lender, reported that quarterly profits fell 33%. The company also slashed its full-year earnings outlook as a result of rising default rates caused by a housing market slump. At the same time DuPont Co., the third-biggest American chemical maker, reported its steepest decline in two years after sliding home sales reduced demand for paint and countertops.

The second day (9/18/2007) was a mirror image of the first. U.S. equity markets rallied sharply, with the Dow Jones

Industrial Average rising more than 200 points after the Federal Open Market Committee cut the federal funds rate a surprising 50 basis points. Financial analysts and economists had generally anticipated a 25-basis-point cut; the larger-than-expected adjustment was widely viewed as positive for both the economy and financial markets. Moreover, the impact on financial markets was dramatic because the federal funds rate had not been reduced in more than 4 years. Coincident with the rate-change surprise was news that the House of Representatives had just voted to allow the Federal Housing Administration, which insures mortgages for low- and middle-income borrowers, to back refinanced loans for tens of thousands of borrowers who were delinquent on payments. The delinquencies resulted from mortgages reset to sharply higher rates. Both news items were clearly inflationary—the dollar fell sharply and gold futures soared to a 27-year high. Finally, the positive news of the day was capped by stronger-than-expected earnings from Lehman Brothers.

Table 2.16 contains price-change data for 17 stocks/exchange traded funds for both days. Although comparisons will be based on standard deviations, percent change for each record is also displayed. The 17 equities were chosen from a population of 200 using the very same clustering methodology described in this section. As we shall see, the stocks can be segmented into 4 distinct subgroups.

TABLE 2.16 *Price-change responses of 17 stocks/exchange traded funds to 2 sets of market conditions. Changes are displayed in both standard deviations and percent.*

	Standard Deviations		% Change	
	7/24/2007	9/18/2007	7/24/2007	9/18/2007
AAPL	-3.34	0.62	-0.0613	0.0181
AIG	-2.86	2.53	-0.0166	0.0289
APC	-2.33	2.54	-0.0334	0.0298
BA	-0.42	-0.14	-0.0023	-0.0017
COP	-2.02	2.34	-0.0385	0.0361
CVX	-2.48	2.05	-0.0294	0.0265
EEM	-2.53	2.46	-0.0319	0.0484
EFA	-2.08	2.49	-0.0151	0.0325
GOOG	0.20	2.01	0.0029	0.0190
LLY	0.00	2.15	0.0000	0.0213
MDY	-2.40	2.46	-0.0187	0.0275
MRO	-2.99	0.81	-0.0518	0.0229
UNH	-0.23	0.29	-0.0033	0.0030
UPS	0.32	2.74	0.0019	0.0195
WMT	-0.19	2.40	-0.0019	0.0259
XLE	-2.41	2.08	-0.0289	0.0303
XOM	-2.59	2.00	-0.0278	0.0280

As before, we can create a visual representation of Table 2.16 by mapping the data to a 2-dimensional grid. The results are displayed in Figure 2.5. For each row in the table, the 7/24 price change is measured on the x-axis and the 9/18 price change on the y-axis. Intersections are recorded as points on the grid.

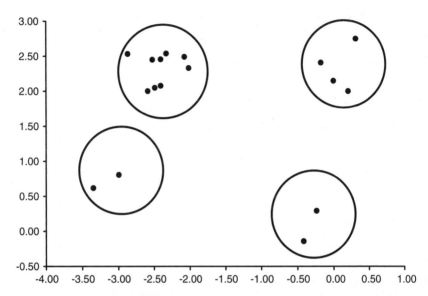

FIGURE 2.5   *Scatterplot composed of price changes for 17 stocks. Each point represents the intersection of an x-axis value (7/24/2007 price change) and a y-axis value (9/18/2007 price change). All values measured in standard deviations against the most recent 20-day volatility window.*

Four distinct clusters are visible in the figure. More than half of the records are located in the upper-left corner, where 7/24 involved a price decrease greater than 2 standard deviations and 9/18 had an equivalently large increase. The lower-left corner contains 2 symbols (Apple Computer and Marathon Oil) that experienced larger decreases on 7/24 but only modest increases (less than 1 StdDev) on 9/18. These stocks significantly underperformed the market during the July–September time frame. More significant are the 4 stocks in the upper right that were immune to the large 7/24 drawdown and rallied substantially on 9/18 with the rest of the market (Google, Eli Lilly, Wal-Mart, United Parcel Service). Bullish investors would be most interested in these stocks, which apparently required little hedging during this time frame. Finally, the 2 stocks in the lower-right corner (Boeing and United Health Group) were relatively immune to the 7/24 drawdown and unresponsive in the 9/18 market rally. Short straddles placed on these stocks during the 7/24 market volatility spike would have been highly profitable.

The importance of comparing price changes in standard deviations rather than the more popular percent change is underscored by the image in Figure 2.6. All other parameters being equal, the figure displays the intersection of the 7/24 and 9/18 price changes measured in percent. Gone are the 4 distinct clusters of Figure 2.5, and in their place is a relatively diffuse continuum of points spanning all areas of the chart.

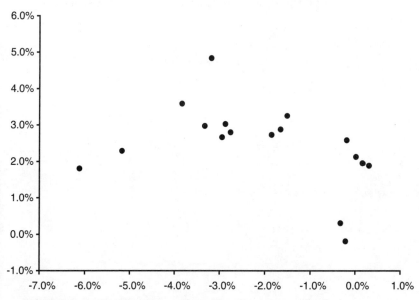

FIGURE 2.6   *Repeat of Figure 2.5 with price changes measured as a percentage of the previous day's closing price.*

This effect is a reflection of the disparities in volatility that are unavoidable in a large population of stocks. A large price change for a volatile stock can be less meaningful than a comparatively smaller price change for a less volatile stock. For example, a 5% price change for $100 stock with 40% volatility is much smaller (2 StdDev) than a 3% price change for a $100 stock that exhibits only 10% volatility (4.8 StdDev). Ignoring underlying volatility effectively scrambles the results by destroying the meaning of the magnitude of the change. Conversely, price changes measured in standard deviations are, in effect, normalized so that direct comparisons have meaning.

This approach became even more meaningful after the housing bubble and banking collapse of 2008. Table 2.17 displays results for a two-day experiment conducted during one of the most volatile time frames in stock market history.

TABLE 2.17   *Second price-change experiment—responses of 16 stocks/exchange traded funds to 2 sets of conflicting market conditions during the 2008 banking collapse. Changes are displayed in both standard deviations and percent.*

	Standard Deviations		% Change	
	2008/09/29	2008/11/24	2008/09/29	2008/11/24
ACL	-2.18	0.12	-0.032	0.006
AMZN	-2.53	1.88	-0.104	0.122
APC	-3.64	1.78	-0.149	0.145
BIDU	-2.39	0.23	-0.113	0.022
BIO	-1.84	0.23	-0.053	0.013
CME	-3.61	1.90	-0.198	0.142
FCX	-2.99	1.51	-0.166	0.134
MDY	-2.78	1.46	-0.071	0.082
MTB	-2.67	1.68	-0.126	0.081
NEM	-0.84	1.02	-0.040	0.094
NKE	-1.15	0.94	-0.040	0.051
RIMM	-1.58	0.16	-0.128	0.010
SOHU	-2.95	1.52	-0.138	0.130
UPS	-0.62	0.93	-0.013	0.044
UTH	-2.51	0.25	-0.059	0.012
WMT	-2.03	-0.08	-0.037	-0.003

The first day (9/29/2008) was characterized by the steepest single-day decline on record, with the Dow closing down 7% and the S&P 500 falling 8.8%. The collapse occurred after Congress rejected a $700 billion bank rescue plan aimed at stabilizing the U.S. financial system.

The second day (11/24/2008) was a mirror image of the first. The Dow climbed 400 points after the U.S. government announced that it would financially rescue Citigroup and assume the risks associated with hundreds of billions of dollars in potential losses. November 24 was also the second consecutive up day after two months of very steep declines that took the Dow from nearly 12,000 to 7,500.

As before, the visual representation contained 4 distinct groups that were closely related in their price-change responses. Results are displayed in Figure 2.7.

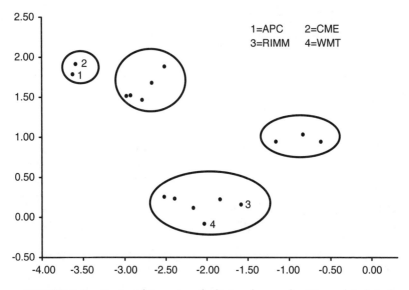

FIGURE 2.7   *Scatterplot composed of price changes for 16 unrelated stocks during the 2008 banking collapse. Each point represents the intersection of an x-axis value (9/29/2008 price change) and a y-axis value (11/24/2008 price change). As before, values are measured in standard deviations against the most recent 20-day volatility window. The legend marks the positions of four of the stocks.*

Four distinct clusters are visible in the figure. The largest includes six stocks that exhibited significant downward price changes on 9/29 but virtually no response to the news of 11/24. Research in Motion and Wal-Mart had the smallest 11/24 price changes, the latter closing slightly down. Conversely, two clusters located in the upper-left quadrant of the chart included stocks that exaggerated the market changes on both days. Most extreme were Anadarko Petroleum (ticker: APC) and the CME Group (ticker: CME). Both were down more than 3.6 standard deviations the first day and up nearly 2 StdDev the second. The tight clustering of these stocks could not have been predicted since they are in completely unrelated industries. (CME operates futures exchanges; Anadarko is an oil and gas exploration company)

As before, the importance of comparing price changes in standard deviations rather than the more popular percent change is underscored by a second image (Figure 2.8) that re-creates the 2-dimensional grid with all price changes displayed in percent. Gone are the 4 distinct clusters of Figure 2.7, and in their place is a relatively diffuse continuum of points spanning all areas of the chart.

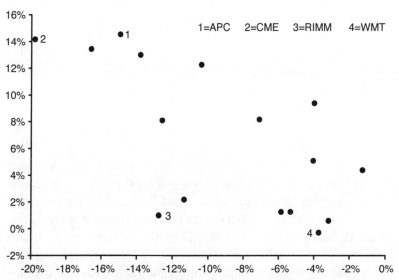

FIGURE 2.8 *Recalculation of Figure 2.7 with price changes measured as a percentage of the previous day's closing price. All evidence of clustering is erased and pairs of stocks that appeared in close proximity in Figure 2.7 are now decoupled.*

Event-based clustering is especially relevant when the goal is to develop a database of historical correlations for predictive purposes. This approach serves as a sharp contrast to more traditional methods such as fundamental analysis or technical charting. An interesting comparison can be made with the science of weather prediction where two basic strategies dominate. The first involves analyzing basic physical principles— cloud physics, thermals, temperature gradients, and so on. The second involves building a database containing historical information about atmospheric parameters and the weather conditions that followed. Using this approach to predict the weather involves searching the database for a set of parameters that correspond closely to those currently being observed. If the theory is correct, the weather will follow the previously observed pattern. Both techniques have some relevance to predicting the performance of stocks. Proponents of the first method often refer to financial metrics, price-earnings ratios, 50-day moving averages, relative strength, stochastics, and the like. The second approach typically employs data mining strategies to identify repeating patterns in historical stock market data.

The previous examples were simplified for clarity. Using the same approach, we could have added many more stocks and at least one additional event. Higher dimensional models representing more than 3 events cannot easily be visualized, and more complex analytical tools must be used to measure the geometric distances between data points. However, it is wise to limit the scope to a small number of very well-characterized events and to construct a database containing a large number of experiments. Hierarchical clustering using Pearson correlation coefficients is a more reasonable approach when the goal is to compare price changes across evenly spaced sequential time frames. That approach is fundamentally different because it measures deviation from the line that defines equivalent price changes for pairs of stocks. The process becomes prohibitively complex for large numbers of stocks because it requires the construction of all pairwise comparisons. Conversely, the method of clustering price changes on a multidimensional grid can accommodate many stocks but few events. Each approach has strengths and weaknesses. It is also important to note that a variety of artificial intelligence methods can be used to create weighting functions to differentiate between closely spaced clusters. This approach often borrows techniques from such diverse areas as molecular biology and particle physics.

Creating Trendlines

Many technical charting strategies rely on moving averages of varying length to characterize the behavior of a stock. Points where different averages cross are often interpreted as triggers for entering or exiting positions. Moving averages can also be used to smooth out spikes and create a simplified representation of a price series. However, more sophisticated techniques can provide a more faithful representation of a dataset while still smoothing out minor fluctuations.

Excel's charting facility includes a trendline tool that supports several modeling options—exponential, linear, logarithmic, power, moving average, and polynomial. The last member of the list, polynomial, is particularly useful for modeling an irregular data series such as a stock price history. Figure 2.9A illustrates this capability with a chart and a 6th-order polynomial trendline for Apple Computer (5/1/2007–9/28/2007). The quality of the fit is apparent when the chart is visually compared to Figure 2.9B, which replaces the polynomial with a 20-day simple moving average.

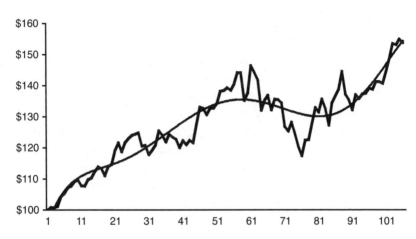

FIGURE 2.9A   *Five months of Apple computer prices (May–Sept 2007)*
superimposed on a 6th-order polynomial-based trendline.
Y-axis = price, x-axis = days.

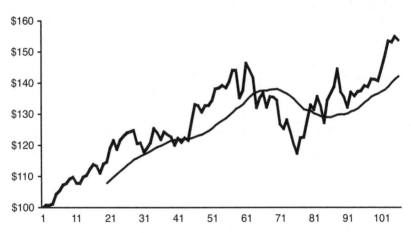

FIGURE 2.9B   *Five months of Apple computer prices (May–Sept 2007)*
superimposed on a 20-day moving average.

The order of the polynomial can be varied to correspond to the number of major fluctuations in the data. A 2nd-order polynomial trendline generally fits a data series with only one hill or valley, 3rd-order fits two fluctuations, and so on. Excel can create polynomials for up to 6 fluctuations. Generally speaking, higher order polynomials provide the most accurate representation for any series because they can accommodate subtle variations in the data.

It is apparent from Figures 2.9a and 2.9b that curve fitting is improved by the more sophisticated approach. However, the moving average fit can be improved at the expense of added noise by reducing the number of days in the interval. Likewise, longer intervals produce a poor but very smooth fit. High-order polynomials provide a fit that is both accurate and smooth. A library of such curves can be used to compare and classify many different charts.

Summary

There is no single correct way to construct a data infrastructure for managing the kind of information we are interested in. Spreadsheets offer advantages with regard to their numerical and statistical capabilities, and calculations that are complex to program in a database can often be accomplished with a single instruction in a spreadsheet. Statistical correlations and certain types of date arithmetic are notable examples. Spreadsheets also have the advantage of being able to solve many complex problems without any programming. Excel has wide variety of functions, and the limitations for their use are surprisingly large—an individual cell can contain 32,767 characters, and a single function can have as many as 255 arguments. It is often possible to construct a statement composed of several functions and numerical calculations in a single cell, and to copy and paste that cell thousands of times with just a few mouse clicks. Finally, spreadsheets provide enhanced graphics capabilities that support data visualization. These features can facilitate comparisons between large numbers of stocks that are grouped into clusters in two or three dimensions.

Conversely, databases can grow much larger than spreadsheets. They can also integrate disparate information sources, including spreadsheets, other databases, and Web pages, into a single data infrastructure. Spreadsheets can be copied and pasted directly into a database in the form of a single table that becomes part of a larger data structure. When the goal is to integrate and manage large amounts of information from many sources, databases are the logical choice. Generally speaking, it makes sense to store large amounts of data in a database and to use query tools like SQL to extract information for export to other applications.

Further Reading

Alexander, M., R. Bovey, S. Bullen, and J. Green, *Excel 2007 VBA Programmer's Reference*, Wrox Press, March 2007.

Chinowsky, Ben, *Getting Started with VBA in Excel 2010*, Microsoft Tutorial available at http://msdn.microsoft.com/en-us/library/ee814737.aspx.

Devore, Jay L., *Probability and Statistics for Engineering and the Sciences*, 5th ed., Pacific Grove, CA: Duxbury Press, 1998.

McCall, Robert B., *Fundamental Statistics for the Behavioral Sciences*, 7th ed., Pacific Grove, CA: Brooks Cole, 1998.

Morris, G., *Candlestick Charting Explained*, McGraw-Hill, 3rd ed., March 2006.

Murphy, J., Technical Analysis of Financial Markets (New York Institute of Finance), Prentice Hall Press, January 1999.

Nison, S., *The Candlestick Course*, John Wiley and Sons, 1st ed., May 2003.

Nison, S., *Japanese Candlestick Charting Techniques*, Prentice Hall Press, 2nd ed., October 2001.

Press, W. H., B. P. Flannery, S. A. Teukolsky, and W. T. Vetterling, *Numerical Recipes in C: The Art of Scientific Computing*, 2nd ed., New York: Cambridge University Press, 1993.

Sokal, Robert R., and F. J. Rohlf, *Biometry: The Principles and Practice of Statistics in Biological Research*, 3rd ed., New York, NY: W. H. Freeman, 1994.

Walkenbach, J., *Excel 2010 Power Programming with VBA*, John Wiley and Sons, April 2010.

Walkenbach, J., *Excel 2007 Bible*, John Wiley and Sons, January 2007.

Endnotes

1. LEFT, MID, and RIGHT text functions will identify appropriate portions of items formatted as numbers or text.

2. Excel for Windows was designed around the 1900 date system because it enabled compatibility with other spreadsheets designed to run under MS-DOS and Windows. Excel for the Macintosh was originally based on the 1904 date system because early Macintosh computers did not support dates before January 2, 1904. As a result, 1900 date system serial numbers are larger than their 1904 counterparts by 1,462 days. The difference includes 4 years and 1 day including a single leap day (one of the years has 366 days).

3. Because Item is the default property of the Range object, we do not have to specify Cells.Item(Row, "B").

Chapter 3

Advanced Topics

Introduction

Because of their flexibility and power, spreadsheets have become the general-purpose tool of choice for virtually every investor. In the past, the dividing line between spreadsheets and databases was clearly defined by size limitations. Those lines have become somewhat blurred. Technical analysis experiments involving fewer than one million records are often easier to construct with a spreadsheet than a database. In this regard it is difficult to distinguish between a database table and a worksheet. For example, a set of records that contains the daily open, high, low, close, and volume for all members of the S&P 500 for five years would occupy 630,000 rows—considerably less than Excel's 1,000,000-row limit. Moreover, our simple data table would only use 5 of the 16,384 available columns. There is virtually no limit to the number of calculations and technical indicators that could be added across the sheet using additional columns. These calculations can then be used to test and refine theories about the behavior of the market or individual stocks, and to tune and fit indicators to that behavior.

This approach is distinctly different from the more familiar back-testing strategies available in most trading platforms. It is also much more scientific because it begins with a theory about market behavior and proceeds through various logical steps that ultimately end with the development of a set of indicators and trading rules. Back-testing indicators without first verifying the underlying market behavior is a hit-and-miss process with a very low probability of success. A more logical order involves developing a theory about market behavior; refining the theory through iterative testing and statistical analysis; selecting appropriate indicators; tuning and back-testing; and, finally, developing a trading strategy.

The more popular approach of fitting indicators to the market is flawed for a variety of reasons. Most significant is the "overfitting" problem that occurs when an indicator is optimally tuned against historical data. The problem is especially severe when the data spans a limited amount of time. Unfortunately, it is almost always the case that indicators, regardless of their sophistication, will work in one time frame and not another. Markets are dynamic in the sense that they are driven by economic forces that change rapidly over time. The past few years, for example, have seen markets that were dominated at different times by dollar weakness, dollar strength, a housing bubble, a housing collapse, a banking crisis, skyrocketing oil prices, collapsing oil prices, and both inflation and deflation. Individual company stocks are more dynamic than the broad market because their businesses respond to both the economy and changes in a specific industry.

Some indicators can be retuned to fit changing market conditions and some cannot. In either case, it is important to have a theoretical model that can serve as a predictor of success. The indicators will stop working when market behavior no longer fits the theoretical model. The overall course of events should, therefore, be extended to include an ongoing process of testing for the original market conditions that were used to select and tune indicators. Top-down approaches that begin with indicators and tuning cannot be extended this way because they lack an underlying theoretical framework.

As we shall see in this chapter, Excel is a perfect platform for developing and testing frameworks that describe the market's behavior and for fitting technical indicators to that behavior.

Time Frames

Today's markets are fundamentally different from those of just a few years ago. Most of the change has been driven by the explosive growth of algorithmic trading in very brief time frames—often less than a second. Many of these systems reside on supercomputing platforms that have the additional advantage of being located on an exchange where they benefit from instantaneous access to a variety of data streams spanning several different markets. Just a couple of years before these words were written, large institutions were focused on minimizing data delays with high-speed Internet connections and fiber-optic links. Since then, they have leapfrogged that problem by simply moving their servers to the exchange. The largest customers are even allowed to view market data a few hundredths of a second ahead of retail customers and to decide whether to take a trade before it is shown to the market. The game has evolved into a process of repeatedly generating very small profits in very brief time frames.

These dynamics have made it exceedingly difficult for the investing public to compete in short-term trading. Unfortunately, the technology gap is growing. Powerful institutional trading systems tend to extinguish trends almost immediately—a process that invalidates most technical indicators that can be embedded in a chart. The capability gap between private and institutional investors increases as the trading time frame decreases. This simple fact has far-reaching implications. In the past, short-term trends resulted from the behavior of individual investors. The result has been the evolution of relatively simple indicators based on moving average crosses, momentum, relative strength, and a variety of standard chart patterns with familiar names like pennant, head and shoulders, and teacup with handle. Most of these patterns have little relevance in a time frame that has come to be dominated by high-speed algorithmic trading because they were designed around the behavior of human investors.

Many of these effects tend to cancel over longer time frames, giving way to more dominant long-term trends. An excellent example is the two-year rally in Amazon.com that took the stock from $50 in December 2008 to $175 in December 2010. During this extended time frame, one of the best investment strategies involved using one-day sharp downward corrections as entry points to buy stock. Stated differently, most downward corrections were met with an immediate rally that took the stock to a new high. At the single-minute level, however, this tendency for reversal was mirrored only at the level of extremely large price changes. In

2010, for example, 1-minute downward spikes larger than 0.5% were immediately followed by a reversal 63% of the time. Unfortunately, the data contains only 106 such changes in 98,088 minutes (67 were followed by a reversal). Extremely large single-minute events are too rare, the reversals are too small, and the trading logistics are too difficult to be exploited by public customers.

Excel is an excellent platform for analyzing this type of historical data and formulating theories like the one just mentioned for Amazon. We might, for example, pursue the minute-level strategy by first identifying and flagging each of the large single-minute downward-spike events using simple conditionals and comparisons. The data could then be sorted to create a list containing the events and associated date and time information. The results are very revealing. For example, during the 1-year time frame analyzed at the minute level, only 9 of the 67 reversal events mentioned previously occurred after 2:00 PM. May was the most active month with 20 events, followed by January with 13 and February with 11. There were no such events in March or December. We could continue this analysis by extracting and charting each of the individual events and paying close attention to the preceding chart patterns. In the end, our goal would be to identify a set of conditions that could become the central theme of a trading strategy. The market would eventually extinguish our discovery and the rules would change. Statistical analysis, pattern discovery, and the development of trading strategies is, therefore, an ongoing dynamic process. Our discussion will focus on various strategies that can be deployed in Excel for constructing and testing theories about the behavior of a stock or an index.

Building and Testing a Model

Every trading strategy must begin with a theory about the behavior of a stock or an index. For illustration purposes we will begin with the simple theory mentioned previously that sharp downward corrections in Amazon stock are followed by a relatively strong rally. The time frame being studied spans 2 years ending in December 2010.

Our strategy uses a worksheet where each row contains date and price information in addition to a series of columns where flags are set to indicate the existence of various conditions. For example, the sheet might be organized with date, open, high, low, close, and volume in columns A–F, and columns G–K reserved for a series of tests. If the closing price change exceeds a preset threshold, then a "1" is placed in column G. A flag is placed in column H of the following row if the next price change also exceeds a threshold and the previous column G is marked. Column G can be thought of as marking "up" and column H as marking "up-up" situations—that is, an "up" day followed by a second "up" day. Likewise, columns I and J can be used to mark "down" and "down-down" events. We then sum each of the columns and divide to obtain the percentage of days where up is followed by another up, or down is followed by another down. A simple form of these tests is listed in Table 3.1.

TABLE 3.1 *Arrangement of conditional and logical expressions to evaluate successive price changes where the first change is larger than 1.5% and the second change repeats the direction of the first. Prices shown are for Amazon.com.*

	A	E	G	H
1	Date	Close	Up	Up-Up
2	20100803	122.42		
3	20100804	127.58	=IF(($E3-$E2)/$E2>.015,1,0)	
4	20100805	127.83	=IF(($E4-$E3)/$E3>.015,1,0)	=IF(AND(H3=1,($E4-$E3)/$E3>0),1,0)
5	20100806	128.32	=IF(($E5-$E4)/$E4>.015,1,0)	=IF(AND(H4=1,($E5-$E4)/$E4>0),1,0)
6	20100809	128.83		=IF(AND(H5=1,($E6-$E5)/$E5>0),1,0)

The actual table would have flags set in G3 and H4. These results are visible in Table 3.2, which displays the expanded version of Table 3.1 with flags instead of conditional expressions.

TABLE 3.2   *Expanded version of Table 3.1 with flags set in columns G and H. Prices shown are for Amazon.com.*

	A	B	C	D	E	F	G	H
	Date	Open	High	Low	Close	Volume	Up	Up-Up
1								
2	20100803	120.00	122.87	119.68	122.42	5962926		
3	20100804	123.06	128.47	123.00	127.58	9275063	1	1
4	20100805	126.77	128.00	125.82	127.83	4282297	0	0
5	20100806	126.72	128.40	125.90	128.32	5065977	0	0
6	20100809	128.46	129.93	127.85	128.83	5087069		

We can increase the flexibility of this approach by replacing the hard-coded values for the price-change thresholds in columns G (0.015) and H (0) with references to cells in the worksheet that can be modified to quickly recalculate the entire column. This approach eliminates the need to cut and paste rewritten versions of the statements—an especially helpful improvement in worksheets containing tens of thousands of rows of data. Table 3.3 contains a set of modified statements.

Different conditions can be tested and the entire sheet recalculated simply by changing the values stored in cells I2 and I3. Table 3.3 adds 3 cells at the bottom that contain the sums of columns G and H along with the ratio. Because most tests will involve many hundreds or thousands of rows, it is wise to store these results to the right of the calculations near the top of the sheet. The ($) symbol placed in front of the row and column descriptors makes the formulas portable in the sense that they can be cut and pasted anywhere that is convenient without altering the ranges they refer to. They will ultimately form the basis of a macro-generated table that will display results for a variety of thresholds that the macro will define in cells I2 and I3.

TABLE 3.3   *Arrangement of conditional and logical expressions to evaluate successive price changes in which the first change is larger than the value stored in cell I2, and the second change is larger than the value stored in cell I3. As before, column E (not shown) contains closing prices.*

	G	H	I
1	Up	Up-Up	Cond
2			0.015
3	=IF(($E3-$E2)/$E2>$I$2,1,0)		0.000
4	=IF(($E4-$E3)/$E3>$I$2,1,0)	=IF(AND(H3=1,($E4-$E3)/$E3>$I$3),1,0)	
5	=IF(($E5-$E4)/$E4>$I$2,1,0)	=IF(AND(H4=1,($E5-$E4)/$E4>$I$3),1,0)	
6		=IF(AND(H5=1,($E6-$E5)/$E5>$I$3),1,0)	
500			
501	=sum($G$2:$G$500)	=sum($H$2:$H$500)	=$H$501/$G$501

Tables 3.1–3.3 display the basic approach. In actual practice we would add two additional columns containing information about downward price changes. More elaborate comparisons containing additional columns with statistical measurements are almost always required as well. Table 3.4 extends our example by adding the r-squared (RSQ) function. R-squared is obtained by squaring the result of the Pearson product-moment correlation coefficient (r) that we used in the previous chapter. Although closely related, Pearson and r-squared differ in one significant way: The Pearson correlation is a measure of linear dependence, while r-squared reveals the percent of the variation in one variable that is related to variation in the other. For example, a Pearson value of 0.6 would indicate that 36% of the variation in one variable is related to the other (0.6 squared = 0.36).

R-squared is often used when the goal is to extend the best fit line through a dataset to predict additional points. We will use r-squared in this context as a measure of the predictability of a trend. Two variables need to be set: the length of the window for the r-squared calculation and the threshold that will be used as a conditional to set a flag when a trend is detected.

Our ultimate goal in this analysis will be to discover whether a large daily price change occurring at the end of a detectable trend is likely to be followed by another price change in the same direction. Thresholds need to be set for the size of the first price change, the second price change, and an acceptable value for the r-squared test. As mentioned previously, we'll also need to experiment with the length of the sliding window used to calculate r-squared.

Table 3.4 depicts the structure of a basic experiment built on this theme. It contains a functional outline organized by column. Columns A–F contain daily price information. Column G numbers the records in sequential order. This information is used by the r-squared function, which requires both y and x-axis values. Column E (closing prices) provides the y-axis values, and column G (sequential record numbers) is the x-axis. Simple sequential numbers are appropriate for the x-axis because the records are evenly spaced. Columns H, I, and J contain the core formulas of the experiment. Column H tests r-squared and sets a flag if the calculated value exceeds a preset threshold contained in cell K4 (0.8 in this example). For this experiment the r-squared calculation is based on a window of 5 closing prices. Column I contains the first price-change test. A flag is set in this column when the closing price change exceeds the threshold set in K2 and the adjoining r-squared flag in column H is also set. Column J sets a flag when a price change exceeds the threshold set in K2 and the previous row of column I also has a set flag. In this way columns I and J compare successive price changes. In this particular experiment the threshold for the second price change is 0%. Stated differently, the final flag is set if both price changes are in the up direction and the first exceeds the preset threshold of 1.5%. Because the sequence of tests begins with r-squared, the final flag will not be set unless the previous 5 closing prices fit a relatively straight line that defines a reasonable trend. Column K contains the threshold values for the first price change (K2), the second price change (K3), and the r-squared calculation (K4). Columns L–N represent a single line summary table that stores totals for the two price-change columns and the ratio. When the strategy is finally automated, this location will contain a summary table with successive rows representing different price-change thresholds.

TABLE 3.4   *Column descriptions for a sample experiment. Tables 3.5–3.7 contain detailed formula descriptions.*

Column	Description
A	Date
B	Open
C	High
D	Low
E	Close
F	Volume
G	Index (sequential record numbers for r-squared calculation)
H	r-squared (5-day window, threshold set in cell K4)
I	up (sets flag if r-squared flag set and price change exceeds threshold set in cell K2)
J	up-up (sets flag if first up flag set and second price change exceeds threshold set in cell K3)
K	Cond (condition thresholds: K2 = first price change, K3 = second price change, K4 = r-squared)
L	up_tot (sum of flags set in column I)
M	up-up_tot (sum of flags set in column J)
N	ratio (M2 / N2)

Tables 3.5–3.7 provide detailed descriptions of the worksheet's layout and formulas. The sheet has been divided into 3 tables to accommodate space limitations of the printed page. Columns E, G, H, and K are included in Table 3.5 which is intended to cover the r-squared calculation. Table 3.6 displays the first and second price-change tests (columns I, J). Associated data columns E (closing prices) and K (preset thresholds) have been omitted for space reasons—the printed page is simply not wide enough. Table 3.7 displays the formulas for the sums (columns L, M, N).

TABLE 3.5   *R-squared calculation (column H) and associated data columns (E, G, and K) described in Table 3.4.*

	E	G	H	K
1	Close	Indx	RSQ	Cond
2	117.13	1		0.015
3	116.86	2		0.000
4	117.89	3		0.800
5	120.07	4		
6	122.42	5	=IFERROR(IF(RSQ(E2:E6,G2:G6)>$K$4,1,0),0)	
7	127.58	6	=IFERROR(IF(RSQ(E3:E7,G3:G7)>$K$4,1,0),0)	
8	127.83	7	=IFERROR(IF(RSQ(E4:E8,G4:G8)>$K$4,1,0),0)	
9	128.32	8	=IFERROR(IF(RSQ(E5:E9,G5:G9)>$K$4,1,0),0)	
10	128.83	9	=IFERROR(IF(RSQ(E6:E10,G6:G10)>$K$4,1,0),0)	
•	•	•		
•	•	•		
500		499	=IFERROR(IF(RSQ(E500:E496,G500:G496)>$K$4,1,0),0)	

The formula contained in column H is composed of 3 pieces. It includes an r-squared calculation wrapped in a conditional statement that in turn is wrapped in an IFERROR statement. IFERROR is required because the r-squared calculation can generate a divide-by-zero error if all prices in the calculation window are the same. IFERROR will automatically set the flag to 0 in rare instances where this situation occurs.

The innermost statement generates a value for r-squared using a window of 5 closing prices. In this example, the range includes cells E2–E6:

```
RSQ(E2:E6,G2:G6)
```

Wrapping the r-squared test in a conditional allows us to set a flag if the value exceeds a threshold. In this case the threshold is stored in cell K4:

```
IF(RSQ(E2:E6,G2:G6)>$K$4,1,0)
```

The final enhancement wraps the conditional in an error-handling construct that sets the flag to 0 in situations where RSQ is undefined:

```
=IFERROR(IF(RSQ(E2:E6,G2:G6)>$K$4,1,0),0)
```

This method of building up complex statements from the inside out is a critical skill and a distinct advantage of Excel's technology. The size and complexity that can be obtained far surpasses anything that would be required for this type of experiment. We could, for example, condense all three test columns into a single complex entity—Excel would have no problem with that level of nesting. In Excel 2010, for example, 64 `IF` functions can be nested as `value_if_true` and `value_if_false` arguments in a single statement. This capability allows the construction of very elaborate scenarios using many fewer columns than one might expect.

Table 3.6 displays a snapshot of the two rows used to test for sequential up price changes. Note that the first test (column I) begins in the fifth data row (row 6) to accommodate the r-squared window. The second test (column J) begins one row later because its result depends, in part, on whether a flag is set in the previous row of column I. Stated differently, the result in J7 builds on the result in I6.

TABLE 3.6   Sequential price-change tests (columns I, J). Associated data columns E and K have been omitted to accommodate the page width.

	I	J
	Up	Up-Up
1		
2		
3		
4		
5		
6	=IF(AND($H6=1,($E6-$E5)/$E5>$K$2),1,0)	=IF(AND(I6=1,($E7-$E6)/$E6>$K$3),1,0)
7	=IF(AND($H7=1,($E7-$E6)/$E6>$K$2),1,0)	=IF(AND(I7=1,($E8-$E7)/$E7>$K$3),1,0)
8	=IF(AND($H8=1,($E8-$E7)/$E7>$K$2),1,0)	=IF(AND(I8=1,($E9-$E8)/$E8>$K$3),1,0)
9	=IF(AND($H9=1,($E9-$E8)/$E8>$K$2),1,0)	=IF(AND(I9=1,($E10-$E9)/$E9>$K$3),1,0)
10	=IF(AND($H10=1,($E10-$E9)/$E9>$K$2),1,0)	=IF(AND(I9=1,($E10-$E9)/$E9>$K$3),1,0)
•	•	•
•	•	•
500	=IF(AND($H500=1,($E500-$E499)/$E4999>$K$2),1,0)	=IF(AND(I499=1,($E500-$E499)/$E499>$K$3),1,0)

Each of the formulas is composed of a single logical comparison using Excel's AND function. The formula in column I verifies that a flag was previously set for the r-squared test while also verifying that the current price change exceeds the threshold defined in cell K2. If both these conditions are met, a slag is set in column I. The formula in column J builds on this comparison by verifying that a flag has been set in the previous row of column I and that the current price change exceeds the threshold value of cell K3. Column J completes the 3-step comparison.

The design of the formula in column I is relatively straightforward. The innermost portion is the logical comparison that includes a verification of the r-squared flag and a price change exceeding a preset threshold measured as a percentage:

```
AND($H6=1,($E6-$E5)/$E5>$K$2)
```

Unfortunately, the AND function returns a value of TRUE or FALSE. Because our ultimate goal is to sum the number of occurrences, we need to replace TRUE with 1 and FALSE with 0. Wrapping the AND comparison with an IF statement solves this problem:

```
=IF(AND($H6=1,($E6-$E5)/$E5>$K$2),1,0)
```

Column J contains a similar formula in the sense that it uses the AND wrapped in IF construct. However, as mentioned above, the AND function refers to both the current price change ($E7-$E6)/$E6 and the flag from the first price change ($I6):

```
=IF(AND(I6=1,($E7-$E6)/$E6>$K$3),1,0)
```

Table 3.7 completes the series with 3 cells that form the basis for a summary table containing many rows. However, in this example we are only testing one set of conditions—RSQ > 0.8 for a window that includes 5 closing prices capped by an upward price change greater than 1.5%. Our summary will count the number of such events and the percentage of occurrences that are immediately followed by a second upward price change.

TABLE 3.7   *Tabulation of final results in columns L, M, and N.*

L	M	N
Up Tot	Up-Up Tot	Ratio
=sum(I2:I500)	=sum(J2:J500)	=M2/L2

The summary is based on a table with 499 rows of data. Many analyses are far larger. For example, a year of minutes contains more than 98,000 rows, and tick-level data can quickly grow to hundreds of thousands of rows. Excel is perfectly suited to testing such models because it can accommodate 1,048,576 rows and 16,384 columns in a single worksheet.

Automating the Process

The previous example was designed to illustrate the basic logic and design of a worksheet that can be used to sequentially compare data items and tabulate the results. The real-life experiment described previously for Amazon.com stock would have yielded disappointing results. For the 2 years ending on December 14, 2010, there were 33 events that met the criteria and 15 were followed by a second price change in the same direction. Since the complete dataset included 504 days, 33 events represents 6.5% or just over 1 trading day per month. Half were followed by an up day and half by a down day. Surprisingly, raising the r-squared requirement to 0.8 had no effect. Stated differently, very large price changes that occur during a statistically significant trend cannot be used to predict short-term direction of the stock. Further increasing the price-change threshold or the r-squared isn't helpful because the number of events falls to a level that is statistically insignificant. A complete set of results for the experiment is presented in Table 3.8.

TABLE 3.8 *Experimental trend-following results for 2 years of daily price changes ending in December 2010 for Amazon.com. In each instance, the first price change exceeds the threshold listed in column 1, and the r-squared of the previous 5 days was larger than 0.8. The column labeled "Up_Up" counts the number of secondary price changes that followed in the same direction. Even the largest price changes were not useful leading indicators.*

Price Change #1 Threshold	Up	Up_Up	Up_Up Ratio
0.000	67	33	0.493
0.001	65	32	0.492
0.002	63	30	0.476
0.003	61	28	0.459
0.004	57	25	0.439
0.005	54	23	0.426
0.006	52	22	0.423
0.007	49	20	0.408
0.008	47	19	0.404
0.009	41	18	0.439
0.010	38	18	0.474
0.011	36	17	0.472
0.012	35	17	0.486
0.013	35	17	0.486
0.014	33	15	0.455
0.015	33	15	0.455

Discovering a distortion that can be profitably traded is always difficult and time consuming. The previous experiment was step #1 in a long iterative process. Excel is an excellent platform for this kind of work because much of the process can be automated. The most efficient style of automation is a kind of hybrid where a VBA program iteratively modifies key parameters in a worksheet that are used to trigger a recalculation. After each round of calculations, the program fetches the results and uses them to populate a summary table. The process continues until a preset endpoint is reached. Many simultaneous experiments can be run using a variety of different parameters and rules. When all the results are collected, the data can be mined for subtle statistical distortions that can be exploited as trading opportunities. The most common scenario involves a promising discovery that is used to trigger more complex experiments and ultimately the selection of a set of indicators.

Listing 3.1 displays a short program that is designed to work with the kind of worksheet described previously in Tables 3.4–3.8. This program and the worksheet that will be described were used to discover entry points for purchasing Amazon.com stock during 2010.

LISTING 3.1   *Sample Excel VBA program for processing trend statistics of the form presented in Tables 3.1–3.8.*

```
1: Sub TrendStat()
2: 'columns: A=Date, B=Time, C=Open, _
       D=High, E=Low, F=Close, G=Volume
3: 'columns: H=Test#1, I=Test #2A, _
       J=Test #2B, K=Test#3A, L=Test#3B

4: On Error GoTo ProgramExit
5: Dim DataRow As Long
6: Dim SummaryRow As Long
```

```
 7: Dim Param1 As Double
 8: Dim Param2 As Double
 9: Dim Start_1 As Double
10: Dim End_1 As Double
11: Dim Step_1 As Double

12: 'summary table headings
13: Cells(1, "P") = "Param1"
14: Cells(1, "Q") = "Param2"
15: Cells(1, "R") = Cells(1, "I")
16: Cells(1, "S") = Cells(1, "J")
17: Cells(1, "T") = Cells(1, "J") & " Avg"
18: Cells(1, "U") = Cells(1, "K")
19: Cells(1, "V") = Cells(1, "L")
20: Cells(1, "W") = Cells(1, "L") & " Avg"

21: DataRow = 2
22: SummaryRow = 2

23: 'set loop parameters here
24: Start_1 = 0
25: End_1 = 0.02
26: Step_1 = 0.001

27: For Param1 = Start_1 To End_1 Step Step_1
28: 'set param2 options here
29: 'Param2 = Param1
30: Param2 = 0
31: Cells(2, "N") = Param1
32: Cells(3, "N") = Param2
33: Cells(SummaryRow, "P") = Param1
34: Cells(SummaryRow, "Q") = Param2
35: Cells(SummaryRow, "R") = Cells(1, "Y")
36: Cells(SummaryRow, "S") = Cells(1, "Z")
37: Cells(SummaryRow, "T") = Cells(1, "AA")
38: Cells(SummaryRow, "U") = Cells(1, "AB")
39: Cells(SummaryRow, "V") = Cells(1, "AC")
```

```
40: Cells(SummaryRow, "W") = Cells(1, "AD")

41: SummaryRow = SummaryRow + 1
42: Next Param1

43: ProgramExit:
44: End Sub
```

In this particular version of the program, columns H–L house the test formulas, column M provides the sequentially number index used for the r-squared calculation, and column N contains price-change thresholds (Param1, Param2) as well as the r-squared threshold that will be used for calculations in column H. The summary table is located in columns P–W, and final statistics for each round of calculations are stored in columns Y–AD.

The program differs from the example outlined in Tables 3.1–3.7 in that it has been extended to test a second set of conditionals. Whereas the previous example tested for a single trend-following case encoded in the formulas of columns I and J, the current program assumes that a second set of conditionals will be encoded in columns K and L. Assuming that columns I and J code the up-up example, columns K and L would most likely code the down-down case. Conversely, the formulas of columns I–L could easily be rewritten to screen for reversals—that is, up followed by down (up-down) and down followed by up (down-up). Moreover, the tests may be reversed in this way without altering the program as long as the original column structure remains intact. In either event, both tests prefilter the dataset using the r-squared calculation of column H.

The flow logic of the program is relatively simple. Lines 24, 25, and 26 contain the boundary conditions for the first price-change test in terms of starting point, end point, and step size. The major program loop begins in line 27. Values for the second price-change test are defined in lines 29 and 30. If line 29 is commented out, the second price change will be set at 0 (any size change). If line 30 is commented out, the second price change will be set equal to the first for every test. One, but not both, of the lines must execute.

Each round of calculations begins by incrementing the first price-change test threshold (Param1) and setting the second price-change threshold (Param2) according to the rules specified (lines 29–30). The new settings are stored in column N of the worksheet, triggering a global recalculation. When the worksheet recalculates, it automatically stores new sums for columns I, J, K, and L at the top of the sheet in Y1, Z1, AB1, and AC1. AA1 and AD1 contain the ratios. Lines 35–40 of the program copy these values to the next line of the summary table. Line 41 increments the row pointer for the table, and line 42 restarts the for loop at the top with the next price-change threshold.

Each time the loop restarts, new price-change thresholds are stored in column N, triggering a global recalculation, and the sums representing the number of flags set in columns I, J, K, and L are automatically stored in Y1, Z1, AB1, and AC1, along with the ratios in AA1 and AD1. The program continues fetching these values and adding them to the growing summary table until the endpoint of the loop is reached. Each iteration of the program is, therefore, equivalent to manually changing the threshold values stored in column N and then immediately cutting and pasting the new sums and ratios from Y1 to AD1 to a new line of the summary table.

Sample Results

Several adjustments and iterations of this particular version of the program were used to evaluate daily price-change dynamics for Amazon.com during the two-year period ending in December 2010. While large upward price changes were not predictive events, large downward price changes were. However, rather than being confirmations, large downward spikes that occurred during a significant downtrend most often signaled the beginning of a reversal. The effect vanishes, however, when the downward price change is not part of a distinct trend. The r-squared test was, therefore, critical to the evaluation. Table 3.9 contains results for the "down_up" scenario. As before, the evaluation included a relatively high r-squared threshold of 0.8.

TABLE 3.9   *Downward trend-reversal test results for 2 years of daily price changes ending in December 2010 for Amazon.com. In each instance, the first price change exceeds the threshold listed in column 1, and the r-squared of the previous 5 days was larger than 0.8. The column labeled "Dwn_Up" counts the number of secondary price changes that followed in the opposite direction.*

Price Change #1 Threshold	Down	Dwn_Up	Dwn_Up Ratio
0.000	52	34	0.654
0.001	49	32	0.653
0.002	47	31	0.660
0.003	43	29	0.674
0.004	40	26	0.650
0.005	38	25	0.658
0.006	36	24	0.667
0.007	34	22	0.647
0.008	30	20	0.667
0.009	29	19	0.655
0.010	25	18	0.720
0.011	23	17	0.739
0.012	21	15	0.714
0.013	17	12	0.706
0.014	16	12	0.750
0.015	15	12	0.800

The table reveals that 23 large downward price spikes (>1.1%) meeting the r-squared test occurred during the 24 months evaluated. A large proportion of these (17) were followed by a reversal. The last entry in the table is more impressive but the frequency is relatively small (15 events in 24 months). However, it is important to note that entering the market 15 times in 24 months with an 80% success rate would result in an extraordinary return. These dynamics need to be balanced against investment goals and personal time frames.

The importance of the r-squared trend significance test is revealed in Table 3.10, which traces results for the 1.1% line of the table across a range of r-squared values from 0.0 (no threshold) to 0.8 (the filter used in Table 3.9).

TABLE 3.10   *Downward trend-reversal test results for 2 years of daily price changes ending in December 2010 for Amazon.com. Each line of the table displays a result of the "down_up" scenario in which the first downward price change was larger than 1.1% and the r-squared filter was set at the level noted in column 1.*

RSQ	Price Change #1 Threshold	Down	Dwn_Up	Dwn_Up Ratio
0.80	0.011	23	17	0.739
0.70	0.011	46	30	0.652
0.60	0.011	58	37	0.638
0.50	0.011	66	40	0.606
0.40	0.011	74	45	0.608
0.30	0.011	87	50	0.575
0.20	0.011	102	58	0.569
0.10	0.011	108	61	0.565
0.00	0.011	134	75	0.560

Our goal in this experiment was to identify a simple set of rules that can be used to pick entry points for purchasing stock. Using these results, we have determined that it is best to initiate long positions on Amazon when the stock declines more than 1.1% at the end of a significant downward trend where r-squared is greater than 0.8. This approach is fine for persistent long positions that are kept open for long periods of time. However, if our goal is to trade the stock by entering and exiting trades in relatively short time frames, then we need to continue studying price-change statistics to identify exit points. We would be looking for situations where an uptrend is followed by a significant reversal. Once again, the correct approach would be to formulate and test theories until statistically significant results are uncovered. These results must then be developed into a trading plan.

Table 3.11 displays the results with a gap of 5 trading days between the first price change and the second. The effect clearly fades, with the difference being largest for small price changes. For example, in the case of downward spikes larger than .001 (line 2 of tables 3.9 and 3.11), the chance of a reversal was 65.3% in the 1 day time frame but only 53.1% in the 5 day time frame. One interpretation would be that a relatively small downward spike during the course of a downtrend is unlikely to completely disrupt the trend and trigger a long-term reversal in the form of regression to the mean. At the practical trading level it could be said that the down spike is too small to trigger a short covering rally. The fading effect is also apparent in the large price-change categories. Across the range from 0% to 1.5%, the average difference between down_up ratios is substantial (11.7%). These results would indicate that during the 2-year time frame evaluated, significant downtrends tended to end with a single large down spike, and that the reversal that followed tended to fade over the next few days. At the end of 5 days, the chance of the stock trading higher was less than it was the very next day.

TABLE 3.11   *Downward trend-reversal test results for 2 years of daily price changes ending in December 2010 for Amazon.com. In each instance, the first price change exceeds the threshold listed in column 1, and the r-squared of the previous 5 days was larger than 0.8. The column labeled "5-Day Dn_Up" counts the number of secondary price changes that followed in the opposite direction 5 days later.*

Price Change #1 Threshold	Down	5-Day Dn_Up	5-Day Dn_Up Ratio
0.000	52	26	0.500
0.001	49	26	0.531
0.002	47	25	0.532
0.003	43	23	0.535
0.004	40	21	0.525
0.005	38	21	0.553
0.006	36	21	0.583
0.007	34	20	0.588
0.008	30	18	0.600
0.009	29	18	0.621
0.010	25	16	0.640
0.011	23	16	0.696
0.012	21	14	0.667
0.013	17	12	0.706
0.014	16	12	0.750
0.015	15	11	0.733

The most obvious question is whether the trend reversal persists beyond the next day. We can answer this question by once again adjusting the formula and recalculating the worksheet. The entire process takes just a few seconds. Table 3.12 reveals the details for a 2-day gap.

TABLE 3.12   *Downward trend-reversal test results for 2 years of daily price changes ending in December 2010 for Amazon.com. In each instance, the first price change exceeds the threshold listed in column 1, and the r-squared of the previous 5 days was larger than 0.8. The column labeled "2-Day Dn_Up" counts the number of secondary price changes that followed in the opposite direction 2 days later.*

Price Change #1 Threshold	Down	2-Day Dn_Up	2-Day Dn_Up Ratio
0.000	52	29	0.558
0.001	49	28	0.571
0.002	47	27	0.574
0.003	43	25	0.581
0.004	40	22	0.550
0.005	38	22	0.579
0.006	36	21	0.583
0.007	34	19	0.559
0.008	30	17	0.567
0.009	29	17	0.586
0.010	25	15	0.600
0.011	23	15	0.652
0.012	21	13	0.619
0.013	17	12	0.706
0.014	16	12	0.750
0.015	15	11	0.733

Results were similar in that the reversal was strongest the day immediately after the large downward price change. Across the full range from 0% to 1.5% the difference between the 1- and 2-day results was still significant (11.4%). As in the 5-day case, every size category displayed evidence of a fading trend. These results would argue that the best strategy involves buying the stock immediately after a large downward price spike at the end of a significant trend, and selling the stock the very next day after the reversal that presumably results from a brief short covering rally.

Building an actual trading system requires additional analysis at the individual event level. For example, we have not yet quantified the average size of the price reversals, and none of the daily price-change analysis provides detail that can be used for intraday trade timing. One solution is to rewrite the formula in column L so that it stores the actual price change rather than a simple flag. The threshold for the first price change (N2) can then be manually set to a high level such as 1.1%, and the recalculated worksheet can be sorted by the magnitude of the result in column L (the size of the reversal). The form of the rewritten column L statement would be this:

```
=IF(AND(K6=1,($F7-$F6)/$F6>$N$3),($F7-$F6)/$F6 ,0)
```

Following these steps for the downward price spikes larger than 1.1% yielded important results. Of the 17 reversals observed, 13 were larger than 1%, with the average 1-day close-to-close increase being 1.8%. Buying at the market close on the day of the down spike generated a larger return than buying at the open on the following day. Moreover, buying at the next day's open yielded slight losses in 2 of the 17 reversal cases because the reversal took place immediately. These dynamics tend to confirm the short-lived nature of sharp reversals in a downtrend—further evidence that they are driven by short covering rallies.

A more detailed minute-by-minute review of each of the 17 reversal days did not reveal any particular pattern that could be used to further optimize the trade. In virtually every case, selling at the high of the day would have yielded a significant enhancement over the close (average enhancement = 0.83%). However, the precise timing of the daily high was difficult to predict. The results are summarized in Table 3.13.

TABLE 3.13   *Summary data for reversal days following downward spikes larger than 1.1%. The column labeled "Close-Close" displays the return that would be achieved by purchasing the stock at the previous day's close and selling at the close on the reversal day. "Open-Close" refers to buying at the open of the reversal day and selling at the close.*

Date	Close-Close	Open-Close	Sell at High Enhancement
20090115	6.08%	6.06%	1.54%
20100510	5.05%	1.20%	0.70%
20090518	3.19%	2.91%	0.01%
20091210	3.10%	2.24%	0.60%
20100521	2.51%	4.10%	1.83%
20090708	2.29%	1.18%	0.74%
20100625	2.26%	2.42%	0.63%
20100825	1.86%	2.42%	0.41%
20090619	1.67%	0.99%	0.60%
20100908	1.40%	0.88%	0.40%
20101102	1.25%	0.53%	0.81%
20091218	1.24%	0.45%	0.24%
20090504	1.03%	-0.61%	1.98%
20090617	0.61%	0.18%	2.00%
20091120	0.52%	1.49%	0.25%
20090903	0.41%	0.09%	0.64%
20091022	0.03%	-0.22%	0.70%
Average	2.03%	1.55%	0.83%

The analysis would not be complete unless we also reviewed the 6 events in which a large downward spike did not result in a reversal. A simplification of the column L statement allows us to capture every event in which a large downward spike occurred on the first day (column K). The following statement stores the second-day price change in column L:

```
=IF(K6=1,($F7-$F6)/$F6,0)
```

In each case, the downward trend continued with a significant drop in price. Buying at the close of the first day and selling at the close of the second resulted in an average loss of 2.16%. Surprisingly, however, closing the trade at the high of the second day resulted in an overall profit. Minute-by-minute review of each event revealed a startling trend—each of the losing days on which the downtrend continued reached a high point in the first half-hour of trading. Selling within the first half-hour would have resulted in an average profit of 0.95%. Stated differently, each down spike was followed by a sharp reversal, with 6 of the 23 events fading almost immediately on the second day. These 6 events ultimately resulted in a loss if the trade was not closed when the stock began falling. Additional minute-by-minute analysis should be used to identify triggers for stopping out of long positions that are initiated in response to the initial drawdown at the close on the first day. Table 3.14 contains relevant data for the failed days on which the stock closed lower after the initial large down spike.

TABLE 3.14   *Summary data for failed reversal days following downward spikes larger than 1.1%. The "Sell at High Enhancement" is surprisingly large for each event and the high point always occurred before 10:00.*

Date	Close-Close	Open-Close	High Minute	Sell at High Enhancement
20100520	-3.92%	-2.39%	9:54	4.42%
20090707	-3.16%	-3.69%	9:34	4.05%
20101001	-2.13%	-2.15%	9:32	2.43%
20100519	-1.34%	-0.73%	9:47	2.68%
20090902	-1.29%	-1.14%	9:51	2.57%
20091217	-1.13%	-1.89%	9:37	2.50%
Average	-2.16%	-2.00%		3.11%

The process of collecting, sorting, and analyzing price-change data is dynamic because the market is in a state of continual flux. Today's trading environment is much too efficient to allow a simple set of rules to persist for any length of time, and significant distortions are always extinguished very quickly. The example used in this chapter was designed to illustrate one of many processes for gaining a statistical advantage. In this regard, a real-life example was chosen to avoid the more common approach of creating a nearly perfect and highly misleading example. Specific technical indicators and chart patterns have been avoided because the goal in this discussion was to build a statistical framework for identifying relevant trends and events. Approaching the problem from the other side— that is, testing and tuning a set of indicators against historical data—is almost always a flawed approach until statistical relevance is established. Once a statistically relevant scenario is identified, however, this approach should become the dominant theme. For Amazon.com we were able to demonstrate a set of conditions that yield statistically advantaged rules for entering and exiting long positions. These rules can be further tuned by deploying other technical indicators once an event is detected. In all cases simplicity should be the major goal.

It is also important to note that any time frame may be chosen for this type of analysis from individual ticks to minutes, hours, days, or weeks. More sophisticated strategies will also include measures of relative performance against other financial instruments or indexes. Today's environment is characterized by virtually limitless amounts of data and powerful analytical tools. Excel is perhaps the most versatile of the group.

I N D E X

FINANCIAL TIMES

In an increasingly competitive world, it is quality of thinking that gives an edge—an idea that opens new doors, a technique that solves a problem, or an insight that simply helps make sense of it all.

We work with leading authors in the various arenas of business and finance to bring cutting-edge thinking and best-learning practices to a global market.

It is our goal to create world-class print publications and electronic products that give readers knowledge and understanding that can then be applied, whether studying or at work.

To find out more about our business products, you can visit us at www.ftpress.com.